Robert A. Broh

MANAGING QUALITY for HIGHER PROFITS

A Guide for Business Executives and Quality Managers

McGraw-Hill Book Company

*New York   St. Louis   San Francisco   Auckland
Bogotá   Hamburg   Johannesburg   London   Madrid   Mexico
Montreal   New Delhi   Panama   Paris   São Paulo
Singapore   Sydney   Tokyo   Toronto*

Library of Congress Cataloging in Publication Data

Broh, Robert A.
  Managing quality for higher profits.

  Includes index.
  1. Quality assurance. I. Title.
TS156.6.B76   658.5′62   81-19292
                                   AACR2

1234567890   DODO   898765432

ISBN 0-07-007975-7

The editors for this book were William Sabin and Christine
Ulwick, the designer was Elliot Epstein, and the production
supervisor was Sally Fliess. It was set in Baskerville by Allyn-Mason,
Incorporated.

Printed and bound by R.R. Donnelley & Sons Company.

To

Jenny for her editorial assistance
Elliott for his interest
Bradley for his examples of subquality offerings
Beckett for her enthusiasm
My parents for their lifelong moral support

ABOUT THE AUTHOR

ROBERT A. BROH has been employed by the Procter & Gamble Company for the past two decades in a variety of management and engineering capacities. He has specialized in manufacturing production, quality systems, and product development, all within his company's consumer and industrial product divisions. Mr. Broh earned the title of Certified Quality Engineer with the American Society for Quality Control, and he holds a master's degree in chemical engineering from MIT. His long experience in the industry eminently qualifies him as a practical expert in the field of quality management.

Contents

Preface

Managing Quality for Higher Profits is written as a guide to help corporate executives and small business managers realize the profits that are available through product quality. It is also written to help quality managers and quality engineers increase their individual productivity and consequently the productivity of their company. The book demonstrates for general managers that the development and maintenance of a productive quality system will significantly embellish the profits of a business and that the failure to accomplish this objective will probably result in the default of substantial profits. It addresses the crucial responsiblity of top management for establishing the solid foundation required to support a quality system capable of generating substantial profits.

Managing Quality for Higher Profits shows that the productivity of a quality system (and of its personnel) can be measured by its contribution to the profits of a business. The proven key for obtaining the maximum profits available via product quality is the development of a quality system which can achieve and maintain the competent design of a product and the process by which it is manufactured (in the case of goods) or delivered (in the case of services). The book identifies and discusses six traits which, when incorporated into a quality system, greatly increase its chances of having this capability. In addition, the book examines the multitude of factors which a capable quality system's managers and engineers must deal with to accomplish a competent product/process design. This discussion provides a quality checklist which can be very useful for helping quality system personnel ensure that a project is managed effectively. The book stresses and demonstrates the critical importance relative to profits of completing the management of these factors prior to the startup of manufacturing or service operations.

Managing Quality for Higher Profits also considers utilization of the total quality cost concept. This concept, or its equivalent, can be a very powerful tool for assisting a quality system in achieving its expected contribution to business profits. It can help direct available personnel to the most attractive quality improvement opportunities, facilitate the allocation of resources for accomplishing justifiable quality improvement projects, serve as a means for obtaining recognition for productive quality system personnel, and substantially aid and expedite decision making.

I hope that you find *Managing Quality for Higher Profits* highly profitable reading.

Robert A. Broh

PART ONE
Quality Expressed in Dollars and Cents

Quality is a very important product characteristic to buyers of consumer and industrial products. Whether we as consumers purchase an expensive new home, an automobile, a television set, or an ice cream cone, or whether an industrial firm buys an expensive computer system, automatic assembly equipment, or just plain pencils for the office, it is almost certain that the quality of the product will be considered, discussed, or cussed. The quality image that is retained in the buyer's mind may very well be a key element in determining if the buyer will purchase additional products marketed by that producer. So, in order to operate a profitable business, a producer must maintain a high level of concern for the quality of his product.

As viewed from a positive perspective, the achievement of outstanding product quality for a high-volume item can contribute tens of millions of profit dollars annually to a company's treasury. This is demonstrated in the case studies in Part III of the book. Even for a lower-volume item, superior product quality can, on a percentage basis, substantially embellish annual company profits. From a negative viewpoint, poor product quality can, in the worst case, deal a fatal blow to a product's chances for success. In this case, all profits which were predicted annually for the product are forfeited. This situation is also exemplified in Part III. Regardless of the viewpoint, product quality can have a very profound repetitive impact on profits. Therefore, product quality must be managed in such a manner that this impact is positive.

1 Quality and the Total Quality Cost Concept

QUALITY DEFINED

I define *quality* as *the degree of excellence at an acceptable price and the control of variability at an acceptable cost*. Let's examine the three key parts of this definition as they apply to a consumer or an industrial product.

Degree of Excellence

A product's degree of excellence is determined by how well its prototype performs the intended function and the advantages the prototype manifests relative to competition. For an example of a product with a very high degree of excellence, we need look no further than the advent of the popular electronic, hand-held calculator. Even in its infancy, the calculator performed the basic mathematical functions efficiently, and it did so much faster and with much greater accuracy than its competition, which consisted mainly of slide rules and adding machines.

Excellence is achieved almost exclusively early in the design phase of a product's life. It is usually characterized by ingenuity and creativity. Unfortunately, there is no proven management technique that yields a high probability that product excellence will be attained. When it is accomplished, the result is a product prototype that functions efficiently and that demonstrates significant advantages versus the anticipated competition. If every potentially salable unit of this product could be manufactured so as to be identical to the prototype, product quality would not need to be a concern beyond prototype design. However, we know that in actual practice this goal is not achievable, particularly in this modern age of high-speed, mass-production facilities. Therefore, we must concern ourselves with product variability.

Control of Variability

Control of variability connotes that a very high percentage of the units manufactured will perform their function as well as the prototype;

3

adhere to safety and regulatory requirements; and not possess defects which are aesthetically displeasing to the extent of portraying an image of shoddy workmanship.

My wife and I bought two identical, intermediately priced stereo units for birthday presents to our twin sons. One of the units performed perfectly. The other unit had a defective turntable arm mechanism, which caused the stylus to skip at the same place on all records. The records played acceptably on the first unit. We exchanged the defective unit for a new one, but it possessed the same defect. Subsequently, we did obtain a stereo which functioned acceptably. Despite the fact that our sons did each obtain a stereo unit which functioned as intended and which they proudly demonstrated to their friends, the 50 percent defective unit rate which we experienced left us with a tarnished image of the quality of products marketed by that company. Given a suitable alternative, we will not purchase additional products marketed by that firm. In net, by failing to control product variability, the company incurred real monetary losses by having to repair or scrap the two defective units, and it also incurred potential monetary losses relative to future sales. If our experience was similar to that of many other buyers of this manufacturer's stereo units, the company may have experienced a very substantial loss of profit due to inferior product quality.

The control of variability is generally believed to be almost entirely the responsibility of the manufacturing organization. This is not true. I once heard an internationally noted quality consultant and teacher state that, based on his many years of investigating quality problems, less than 20 percent were caused by manufacturing error. My personal experience is consistent with his finding. Actually, responsibility for the control of variability must be shared between the product design and manufacturing organizations. However, since manufacturing error is the cause for only a minority of excessive variability occurrences, it follows that effective product design will eliminate the majority of the potential for a product to show undesirable variability. This fact is clearly demonstrated in the case studies of Part III. The control of a product's variability must begin simultaneously with the initiation of design efforts, and it can end only when the product is no longer marketed. The omission or premature termination of even a part of this control carries a risk that a substantial amount of otherwise obtainable profit will not be realized.

Book Objectives

The first of the three main objectives of this book is *to demonstrate that successful control of a product's variability can substantially embellish profits*, and *that failure to control a product's variability can devastate profits*. This is accomplished via the case studies in Part III. The second objective is *to identify and discuss the areas of responsibility that must be effectively managed to obtain control of product variability*. Although their relative importance can differ, these areas of responsibility and the specific factors that comprise each one are basically the same for most industries that are involved in the marketing of a manufactured product. This objective is covered in detail in Part II. Chronologically, the second objective is considered before the first objective in order to facilitate a better understanding of the material presented in Part III. The third objective of the book is *to identify the essential ingredients of quality systems that are capable of effectively controlling these areas of responsibility such that profits are substantially enhanced*. This subject is covered in the latter portion of Part III.

Parts I, II, and III are intended to apply to any industry or business which manufactures a consumer or an industrial product for profit. In reading through Parts II and III you will notice that a majority of the examples presented are from the homogeneous product (e.g., cooking oil, soft drink, shampoo, floor polish, chemicals) industries rather than the discrete product (e.g., furniture, automobiles, electrical appliances) industries. The reason for this is simply that I am personally more familiar with the former type of products and businesses. Actually, so long as a product is being manufactured for profit, the same fundamental principles apply to managing the quality system so that it can contribute handsomely to those profits. The examples presented are only intended to provide clarity and better understanding of the key points. Finally, Part IV is devoted to discussing the major points of Parts I, II, and III as they have application to the service industries.

Money

Money is the third important portion of our quality definition. Given unlimited financial resources, it is highly probable that almost any desired degree of excellence or control of variability could be attained. As an illustration of this point, consider the degree of excellence achieved by the U.S. space program in designing and building space vehicles capable of landing men on the moon and returning them to earth safely. This feat, unequaled even to this day, demonstrates the type of outstanding accomplishment that can be attained when resources are practically infinite. However, in the real world of industry, businesses must be able to realize the profits which motivate them to continue doing business. In order for this to happen, the degree of excellence must be achieved so that the product can be offered at an *acceptable price*, and the control of variability must be attained at an *acceptable cost*. As an example, suppose that you are president of the highly successful Space Age Automobile

Company. Over a 15-year period, you direct $15 billion to your research and development organization to meet the consumer need of inventing and developing an automobile/fuel system such that 100 miles can be traveled at 55 miles per hour for only $0.10 worth of fuel. After 15 years of ingenius and devoted effort, your researchers meet their objective. Your engineers inform you that it will cost an additional $5 billion to construct manufacturing facilities for this product. Then your treasurer informs you that in order just to break even on your investment you will have to price this product at $300,000 and sell 1 million of them. The company achieved an unparalleled degree of excellence, but what are the chances of this venture being profitable? This example may border on the ridiculous, but the point is clear: *product quality must be achieved with limited financial resources*.

THE TOTAL QUALITY COST CONCEPT

Before proceeding further we need to understand the fundamentals of the total quality cost concept. Quality costs include all expenses incurred to control and assess quality and to pay the consequences of inferior quality.

The Cost Categories

Quality costs can be classified into one of three categories:

Appraisal Costs

Appraisal costs are expenses incurred to assess quality. For example, the cost of examining a sample of golf balls from an assembly line in order to be certain that the production represented meets specifications is an appraisal cost. The cost of performing chemical analyses on samples of raw materials to be certain that they adhere to specifications before being used is also an appraisal cost.

Failure Costs

Failure costs are to pay the consequences for inferior quality. They can result from disposing of subquality material; shipping a subquality product into the market; and being unable, because of a quality reason, to manufacture or ship acceptable production. The cost of reworking (disposing of) microwave ovens which were improperly assembled during manufacturing is a failure cost. In the stereo example presented earlier, the manufacturer can decide to repair the two defective units or to scrap them. For either option, the associated costs are because of the shipment of units with substandard quality and are, therefore, classified as failure costs. Another type of failure cost is the expense resulting from litigation initiated by a customer who experiences an injury while using the product. The honoring of product warranties also falls into this cost classification.

A somewhat different but very important type of failure cost is the "cost" of lost profit due to dissatisfied customers who discontinue purchasing the specific product or the marketer's products in general. This can rapidly escalate if the dissatisfaction is communicated to other potential customers. It is difficult to quantify this cost of lost profit. However, a genuine effort should be made to obtain at least a reasonable estimate, because it can be a very substantial cost, even to the extent of being the highest of all quality costs. This topic will be considered in detail in Part III.

Preventive Costs

Preventive costs involve expenses incurred in order to eliminate or reduce appraisal costs or the occurrence of failure costs. Examples are costs to train production personnel in systems and procedures for avoiding the production of defectives. Relating to the stereo example previously described, if the producer assigned a group of people to ascertain the cause of the malfunction and to recommend and institute corrective action to eliminate it, the costs associated with the group's activities would be preventive.

Keeping in mind that preventive and appraisal costs are to control and evaluate quality respectively, whereas failure costs are to pay the consequences of undesirable quality, we are now prepared to examine a model for optimizing quality costs as shown by Figure 1-1.

The Total Quality Cost

The *total quality cost* is the sum of preventive, appraisal, and failure costs. At the far left, the production of many defective units occurs because very little is being spent for preventive and appraisal measures. The result is a high failure cost and, hence, a high total quality cost. As the percentage of defective units decreases (moving to the right on the abscissa) because of preventive and appraisal measures being initiated and increased, the failure cost declines. Most importantly, the *total quality cost also decreases* until X is reached. To the right of X, as the percentage of defective units continues to decrease, the failure cost also continues to decrease, but the *total quality cost increases*. This is because at some point (designated X percentage of defective units) it can become more expensive to prevent further defectives than the cost to tolerate them. X represents

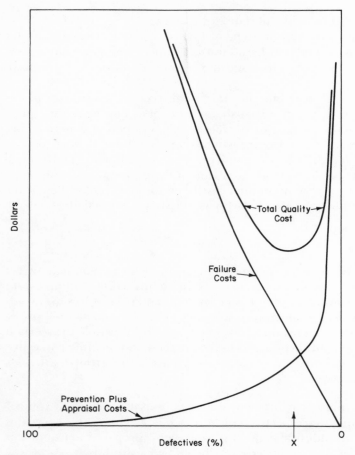

FIGURE 1-1   Model for optimizing quality costs.

the percentage of defective units at which the *total quality cost is a minimum*. The actual percentage of defective units where X occurs depends upon the specific industry and company. However, it is unusual for the minimum to occur at "zero defects," a popular quality objective in the 1960s. For X to occur at zero defects, the product being produced must have a very high unit cost such that the production of even one defective unit can result in a very high failure cost. This situation can be approached in a few industries like those producing highly expensive computer systems or spacecraft. The point of this discussion is simply that *there is an optimum total quality cost. To operate significantly removed on either side of this optimum is to forfeit profits* which can be realized by the efficient management of the quality system.

THE QUALITY SYSTEM

The *quality system* includes all personnel, equipment, and procedures employed for the purpose of controlling product quality. The organization with primary responsibility for managing the quality system is in some companies referred to as the Quality Control Department, whereas in some other companies the same organization is called the Quality Assurance Department. Which is correct? Control implies prevention, and assurance infers appraisal activities relative to the total quality cost concept discussed previously. Therefore, both quality control and quality assurance are included in the quality system. Perhaps an appropriate nomenclature for the organization which manages the quality system would be the Quality Department.

There is also considerable variation and debate regarding the organizational affiliation of the Quality Department. For example, a company with heavy emphasis upon the development of new products, like a new company, might elect to attach quality to the Product Design Organization. At the other extreme, a company with many established and profitable products might choose to affiliate quality with the Manufacturing Organization. In the middle, a substantially strong argument can usually be made that the Quality Department should be an independent organization reporting directly to upper management, so as to eliminate biases. Although the organizational affiliation can influence its efficiency, the fundamental ingredient of any quality system is the people who comprise it. Competent personnel can usually figure out a way to meet objectives despite organizational barriers. Regardless of the organizational title and affiliation, the *primary goal of the quality system should be to optimize the total quality cost so as to maximize the system's contribution to profits.*

PART TWO
Management Responsibilities

This portion of the book is devoted to a discussion of each of the *fundamental areas which require competent management in order to obtain control of product variability*. These areas are:

1. Specifications for the finished product.

2. Specifications for all components.

3. Supplier qualification program for all components.

4. The "recipe." (formual or assembly)

5. Manufacturing operations.

For each area, we shall discuss the numerous *factors* which need to be examined to determine appropriate actions for controlling product variability within that area. The factors presented are not intended to be all-inclusive. They are intended to include the important considerations which are common to most manufacturing operations. However, any specific manufacturing operation must be evaluated for factors that are unique to it.

As we proceed through Parts II and III, it will become evident that "appropriate actions" for controlling the product variability for a specific factor are most effective when they are preventive in nature. When preventive measures prevail, quality failure costs will be theoretically avoided and practically minimized. When appraisal measures are employed as the fundamental tool against excessive quality costs, quality failure costs in the marketplace are minimized, but scrap and salvage costs can be very high. The classic saying, "quality cannot be inspected into a product" is quite true. *Prevention should be the primary quality tool employed in any manufacturing operation*. It will also become evident that these "appropriate actions" can be more economically implemented during the design phase of a product's life than at any other time.

11

2 The Finished Product Specification

PRODUCT SPECIFICATIONS

The first area which must be well managed is the Finished Product Specification (FPS). The FPS consists of all of the product specifications that serve as benchmarks against which routine production is judged to ensure that it is acceptable for shipment. Each product specification applies to a single product attribute, and it consists of appropriate limits and the particular method used to test production against those limits.

Attributes

Product specifications play a very important role in determining the extent to which the components, the recipe, and the operation must be controlled. Therefore, they significantly influence the design and the cost of the entire manufacturing operation. For this reason, the FPS must be carefully and competently developed. A critical factor to be considered for this area is the *determination of the functional, aesthetic, safety, and regulatory product attributes which are of sufficient importance to be a part of the Finished Product Specification.* This can only be accomplished with product knowledge and knowledge about the product user. Technical expertise and market research respectively are required. An example follows for each type of product specification mentioned above for this factor:

1. A functional product specification relates to the ability of the product to perform its intended job. The manufacturer of digital alarm clocks might specify that each clock shall not gain or lose more than 2 seconds during any given 24-hour period.

2. The manufacturer of expensive wooden desks would probably insti-

tute an aesthetic product specification that all exterior surfaces of the desk shall be free of scratches, nicks, and other blemishes.

3. The producer of a new electric baseball game might have a product safety specification that a seal demonstrating that the design is electronically safe be present and legible in a particular location on each game. (Of course, this assumes that use of the seal has been appropriately authorized following satisfactory test results.)

4. The manufacturer of a new automobile might specify that the emissions through the exhaust system must comply with all relevant federal, state, and local laws. This would ensure that regulations were adhered to.

Attribute Limits and Their Test Methods

The second factor for this area is that *for each attribute in the FPS, limits must be defined which include only product known to be acceptable to consumers or users. The test method* to be used in checking product against these limits *must also be defined.* A bias can exist between two test methods used to evaluate the same attribute. Thus, it is imperative that the same test method used to define the limits also be used to judge continuing production against the limits. Together, a set of limits and the respective test method constitute the product specification for one attribute. To establish a product limit without knowledge of the acceptability of the product included is to abdicate control of variability for chance, or, stated otherwise, profits for costs. Product which exceeds a limit may or may not have been determined to be unacceptable. Therefore, an attribute limit signals the starting point for a potential or real consumer, safety, or regulatory concern.

As an example of an attribute limit relating to a potential concern, suppose the producer of a new type of kitchen oven has ascertained via consumer testing that, at temperatures above 300°F, users cannot distinguish between the condition of the prepared food or the time needed to prepare it, even if the temperature deviates from the indicated setting by plus or minus 10°F. This producer then knows that if each unit performs within plus or minus 10°F of the set temperature (above 300°F), users will not be dissatisfied due to inadequate temperature control. The temperature variation at which users can detect significant differences may or may not have been determined. Thus, the product specification for this attribute could be "at temperatures of 300°F and higher, the unit must maintain a temperature of plus or minus 10° of the set temperature." It is important to note that for this example units which do not adhere to the limits are not necessarily unacceptable.

As an example of an attribute limit relating to a real concern, consider a tire manufacturer. Federal regulations specify the minimum bursting strength in pounds per square inch of air pressure that tires must be able to withstand. The actual specified bursting strength depends upon the tire size. Therefore, the manufacturer knows that the tires must adhere to the government's minimum specification for bursting strength for the specific tire size. He or she also knows that if tires do not adhere to the specification, there is a risk of regulatory action against the firm. The risk includes the possibility of a ban of the product for sale in retail and wholesale outlets. Also, there is risk of consumer litigation against the company if even remotely related accidents occur. So, in this example, a minimum burst strength limit could be set with knowledge that tires meeting the requirement are acceptable and with knowledge that tires not meeting the requirement are unacceptable.

The point of this discussion is simply that to control variability, attribute limits must be established with *knowledge* that product meeting those limits is acceptable. When attribute limits are set without this knowledge, it is entirely possible for unacceptable product to be routinely shipped to customers. It will later be shown that this can be a very costly proposition.

Overly Restrictive Limits Can Result in Unnecessary Costs

It can also be expensive to err in the opposite direction. If limits are established which are unnecessarily narrow or otherwise overly restrictive, expensive equipment may have to be purchased to adhere to the pseudo requirements. In addition, large quantities of product which are actually suitable for use may be reworked or even scrapped with the associated significant costs. As an illustration of the way in which overly restrictive limits can amplify costs, consider the effect of a decision as to how a product specification should be expressed.

Target limits are stated as the desired average value plus or minus half the tolerance. The target specification for filling mustard into a jar possessing a labeled weight of 300.0 grams might be written as 300.0 grams plus or minus 4.0 grams. This denotes that it is desirable for the fill weight for any production segment to average 300.0 grams, but individual units with fill weights anywhere between 296.0 and 304.0 grams are acceptable.

Range limits are stated as the tolerable range. The range specification for the mustard example above would be 296.0 to 304.0 grams. This denotes that as long as the average fill weight and individual jar fill weights for any segment of production fall between 296.0 and 304.0 grams, it is not necessary to provide any further fill-weight control.

Although it is quite often astute to choose to use target limits in preference to the corresponding range limits, the decision to do so usually involves money. This is because equipment capable of controlling to a target limit is usually more expensive. Furthermore, some lost production time may be experienced whenever it is necessary to make equipment adjustments so as to direct the average closer to the target value. In the example cited above for the filling of mustard into jars, the target specification of 300.0 plus or minus 4.0 grams would probably be the wise choice. If a range specification is selected, repetitive monetary losses will result from the donation of free incremental product to consumers whenever the average fill weight for a significant quantity of production exceeds 300.0 grams. On the other hand, if the average fill weight is less than 300.0 grams, the mustard producer risks monetary losses through consumer dissatisfaction and/or regulatory action.

For a great number of practical situations, the extra costs associated with target limits are not justifiable, and range limits are entirely adequate. Cap torque is a measure of the effort required to remove a closure from a bottle or jar. Suppose that the mustard producer has ascertained via market research that it is no more difficult for a user to remove from their jars a cap having a torque of 4 inch-pounds than one of 12 inch-pounds. Assume further that the producer has determined that a cap torque of 4 inch-pounds provides a sufficient cap-jar seal to adequately protect the product and that a cap torque of 12 inch-pounds will not break the jar. For this situation, a cap-torque range specification of 4 to 12 inch-pounds would probably be sufficient. Adoption of a target specification of 8 plus or minus 4 inch-pounds would probably involve the absorption of extra costs with no added benefits.

This discussion was not meant to suggest that all attribute limits must be expressed either as a target or a range. Other alternatives, such as a maximum or a minimum limit or unbalanced target limits $\left(\text{e.g., } 8 \begin{smallmatrix} +4 \text{ inch-pounds} \\ -2 \text{ inch-pounds} \end{smallmatrix}\right)$, are possible. The purpose of the discussion is to demonstrate that the choice of the way in which attribute limits are expressed can significantly affect costs. In net, attribute limits must be sufficiently tight for the producer to know that the product needs of the ultimate user will be satisfied, but sufficiently pragmatic so that unnecessary costs will not be incurred.

Overall Design

A third factor in this category is that *overall design must yield the ability to routinely manufacture product which meets all product specifications*. That is, the design of component specifications, the recipe, operations, and equipment must be accomplished so that when each component adheres to its component specification, when recipe and operating instructions are followed, and when all equipment is operating as intended, the resulting manufactured product will automatically comply with the Finished Product Specification. This is not an easy criterion to fulfill because it is quite unusual for all acceptable combinations of components, recipe, operating procedures, and equipment to be tested during product design.

To illustrate, consider a producer of an improved margarine. The producer will probably include a tight finished-product color specification to be certain that the product is attractive to consumers. Suppose that during product design this producer determined that m pounds of a yellow dye per 100 pounds of total margarine formula would give the desired hue. Consequently, he or she specified a fixed dye concentration for each batch of margarine. Problems are not encountered for several months until a shipment of vegetable oil arrives which is somewhat darker in color than previous ones. The margarine made from this oil has the desired consumer attributes for hardness and melting temperature, but the fixed dye concentration yields an unacceptably dark product. For this combination of specified components, operation, and formulation, a product specification could not be satisfied. The producer ends up with product to be salvaged or scrapped. The related failure costs could have been avoided if the dye addition had been specified in increments, each followed by a color check of the batch, until the desired target color was attained. Alternatively, a tighter color specification could have been developed for the vegetable oil so that a fixed dye concentration could be used. However, this approach would have to be accomplished for the other ingredients too.

Disposition of Nonconforming Product

A fourth factor for this area is that *management must determine on an individual basis the disposition of all production not meeting product specifications*. Previously, we discussed that product outside of specifications may or may not have been determined to be unacceptable. In either case, a risk of lost profit exists if the product is shipped. Therefore, for any particular product out-of-specification occurrence, management needs to make a conscious decision to ship, salvage, or scrap the product, or to conduct tests to determine the acceptability of the product before making the decision. Whatever the choice, it must be made considering the intent of the violated specification and the benefit-to-risk ratio of shipping the product; and if the product is shipped, the reason for that decision must be communicated to nonmanagement personnel. The latter is a most important point in that, if nonmanagement personnel do not understand the reason for allowing out-of-specification product to be shipped, they may conclude that the violated specification is not really important. This belief can erode the motivation to perform their function of helping to ensure that the specification is adhered to in the future. If this situation occurs frequently, their general motivation relative to product quality can be destroyed.

To illustrate, assume that a candle manufacturer has a product specification that "candles will not melt at temperatures below 110°F," and that the purpose of this specification is to avoid disfiguration of the candles during shipment and warehouse storage. Samples representing 10,000 candles are found to begin to melt at 100°F. In all other respects the candles are normal. The source of the problem is traced to an impurity in a shipment of a waxy chemical used to formulate this product. Chemical analysis of a sample of this material did not detect the impurity. A new test is developed and instituted to detect the impurity should it recur. Management decides to ship the out-of-specification candles to midwestern locations because it is winter, and there is no real risk of encountering higher temperatures in this region. This represents an intelligent technical and business decision. However, if nonmanagement personnel are not informed as to the reason, they might conclude that the relevant product specification is just not important. Consequently, if the situation does occur again and the new test does detect the impurity, the analyst may not communicate the result to appropriate personnel because he or she believes that the use of such material does produce shippable product. If this occurs in summer, significant failure costs may result.

Control Limits

To conclude this chapter, we'll briefly discuss a technique which can help to prevent the occurrence of out-of-specification production. In many practical cases, the overall operation is capable of tighter control than required by product specifications for consumer acceptability, safety, and regulatory concerns. For this circumstance, control limits can be established to provide an early warning that something has gone out of control before the production of unacceptable product actually occurs. In the kitchen oven example cited earlier, we knew that consumers could not distinguish plus or minus 10°F from the set temperature. Assume the producer has learned that when the components meet specifications and when they are assembled properly, the finished oven temperature never deviates by more than 6°F from the set temperature. A control limit of plus or minus 6°F is set. Then if units are detected which demonstrate a 7°F to 10°F deviation, the producer knows that, although the ovens are entirely suitable for consumers, something abnormal is occurring. Unless he or she is able to identify and correct the abnormal occurrence, the producer may shortly be manufacturing salvage or scrap.

Summary

To summarize:

1. The Finished Production Specification should include a product specification for every important functional, aesthetic, safety, and regulatory product attribute.

2. For every product attribute in the FPS, limits which include only product known to be acceptable to users must be defined. The relevant test method must also be defined.

3. Overall design must be achieved such that when all Component Specifications are satisfied, when recipe and operating instructions are followed, and when equipment operates as expected, the manufactured product will adhere to all product specifications.

4. When a segment of production exceeds product specifications, management must decide on an individual basis the disposition of the production implicated.

3 Components

Components include all items that during manufacturing become a part of a product in its final, shippable form. For a relatively simple product like a bottle of rubbing alcohol, the only components are the chemicals to make the alcohol, the bottle, the cap, the label, and the box used to ship the product. At the other extreme would be the myriad of components required in an automobile assembly operation. This would include the chassis, doors, windows, tires, engine, seats, bumpers, grill, transmission fluid, antifreeze, fenders, radio, hood, interior parts, and so on.

COMPONENT SPECIFICATIONS

In this section, we shall discuss the factors which must be considered for each component in order to determine the particular characteristics which require specification. For a component, all of the individual characteristics specified constitute its Component Specification (CS).

Before starting this discussion, we should note that the reason for establishing the individual specifications in a Component Specification is not restricted to quality considerations. A manufacturer might specify that shipments of an acid be made to his plant in glass-lined trucks because corrosion products would contaminate the acid if it were shipped in trucks with a metal lining. This particular specification protects quality. On the other hand, the same manufacturer might specify that shipments of noncorrosive mineral oil be made to the plant in glass-lined trucks because it is substantially cheaper to purchase the material in bulk than in individual drums. This specification is for cost control. The following discussion deals only with the factors which must be considered in order to control product quality.

Examples

An example of a typical Component Specification for a bulk substance appears in Table 3-1. Assume that this Component Specification has

TABLE 3-1.   Example of a Component Specification for a Bulk Material (Sodium Sulfate)

SODIUM SULFATE
(Na_2SO_4)
COMPONENT SPECIFICATION No. 444

Attribute	Specification	Test method
1. Na_2SO_4 (%)	99.3% minimum	A
2. H_2O (%)	Less than 0.3%	B
3. H_2SO_4 plus (%) HCl	Less than 0.2%	C
4. NaCl (%)	Less than 0.2%	D
5. Iron	Less than 10 ppm	E
6. Heavy metal content	Less than 25 ppm	F
7. Specific gravity	2.65–2.70	G
8. Melting point	880°C–888°C	H
9. Appearance	White crystals	I
10. Odor	None; comparable to standard	J
11. Container	Ship only in 100-pound bags with a polyethylene liner. Each bag must be labeled with the CS number and the chemical name in 1 inch-high letters.	—
12. Age at time of shipment	Less than 3 months old	—

been developed by a glassware producer for the sodium sulfate which is used in one of the company's products. Note that the Component Specification includes a CS number in addition to the component's chemical nomenclature. This is to minimize the probability of error if the glassware manufacturer currently or at some time in the future utilizes more than one grade of sodium sulfate (Na_2SO_4). Sodium sulfate of lesser purity than the 99.3 percent minimum required by CS No. 444 may be acceptable for another product marketed by the same company. For the same reason, it is also wise to insist that every container of the component be identified by this number. The latter need is covered in item 11 of CS No. 444

Sodium sulfate can be produced by several different processes. For CS No. 444, it was assumed that it would be manufactured by reacting sulfuric acid with sodium chloride so as to form sodium sulfate and hydrochloric acid. Subsequently, the Na_2SO_4 must be purified by processes which appropriately decrease the concentration of unreacted sulfuric acid and sodium chloride and by-product hydrochloric acid. Component

Specification No. 444 is written specifically for $\dot{N}a_2SO_4$ produced in this manner. This can be seen by examining items **3** and **4**. Should the glassware producer purchase Na_2SO_4 from a supplier who manufactures this chemical by a different process, a different CS would be needed.

Note that in CS No. 444, most of the attributes pertain to the function (e.g., item **1**), the aesthetics (e.g., item **9**), or the safety (e.g., item **6**) of the sodium sulfate. A letter has been used to designate the test method which applies to each particular component attribute. Each such letter should provide reference to a given test method which defines the exact test procedure to be employed. Also note that item **11** specifies a polyethylene liner inside each bag. This is to avoid moisture absorption by the sodium sulfate during storage and shipment.

Table 3-2 presents a typical Component Specification for a discrete component, the white queen, to be incorporated in a chess game. The recipe and Finished Product Specification for this game are presented in Chapter 4. Again, note that for CS No. 133, most attributes pertain to the function (e.g., item **5**), aesthetics (e.g., item **3**), or safety (e.g., item **6**) of the component.

The development of a Component Specification (and qualified suppliers, discussed in the next chapter) usually involves a significant utilization of resources. However, many times this effort can be substantially simplified when the component is already available in the market. For this situation, if it is determined that the specific component from a given supplier is acceptable, then that supplier's Finished Product Specification for the commodity can serve as the foundation for the required Component Specification. Subsequently, customized packaging and

TABLE 3-2.   Example of a Component Specification for a Discrete Material

QUEEN FOR A CHESS GAME COMPONENT SPECIFICATION No. 133		
Attribute	**Specification**	**Test method**
1. Height	4.95–5.05 centimeters	A
2. Diameter of base	1.95–2.05 centimeters	B
3. Geometry	Must conform with drawing 133a	—
4. Material	Polyethylene	C
5. Color	White; not significantly different from standard	D
6. Appearance	All surfaces smooth and free of imperfections; no sharp edges	E

shipping specifications plus any special specifications need to be added. To develop the CS of Table 3-1, it is entirely possible that the glassware manufacturer, after ascertaining that the vendor's component was suitable for the product, adopted items **1** through **10** directly from the supplier's FPS, and added items **11** and **12** to meet his or her particular requirements.

When the supplier's Finished Product Specification is not sufficiently stringent to meet the producer's needs, at least three alternatives are available:

1. The vendor might agree to alter the manufacturing process so as to produce a product (the customer's component) which does satisfy the customer's needs.

2. The vendor might continue operating his or her manufacturing process with no changes, but agree to select and ship to the customer only those portions of production which comply with the customer's requirements. Obviously, this can only be an option if a sufficient amount of production does adhere to the needed Component Specification.

3. The supplier may decide not to do business with the customer.

The choice for a given situation of this nature will customarily be decided based on the relevant economics. The development of a CS for a component which is not currently available in the market is considerably more complex. The discussion which follows examines the factors that must be considered in order to design a meaningful CS regardless of the status of the vendor's FPS for the component.

Attributes and Limits

When developing a Component Specification, the most important factors to consider are the *attributes which are desired in that component and the respective limits for each attribute*. Attribute specifications are usually established for reasons resulting from *functional, aesthetic, safety, sanitary, or regulatory* considerations.

As examples of items specified for each one of these reasons, take the case of a pancake syrup manufacturer who uses glass bottles as a packaging component. The function of the bottles is to transport the product from the point of manufacture to the consumer. The bottle must have sufficient strength to accomplish this. Therefore, a minimum wall thickness at all locations on the bottle should be specified so that the bottle will not break during packaging and shipping. To help ensure that the product appears aesthetically pleasing on store shelves, the pancake syrup producer will probably specify that the bottles be free of flaws in the glass and meet a requirement for transparency. To ensure customer safety, he or she will insist that the bottles be free of cracks and chips. The syrup manufacturer certainly desires to deliver the product in a sanitary condition to consumers. For this reason it will be specified that the bottles be clean and free of any foreign material. Since regulations exist relating to the quantity of product contained by the package, a specification is necessary for the minimum internal volume of the bottle. The consideration for determining appropriate limits for each attribute are analagous to those discussed for establishing product limits in Chapter 2.

Inspection Methods

The inspection method used to determine whether a component adheres to a particular specification is an extremely important factor. For any particular characteristic specified in the Component Specification, it is imperative that the supplier and the customer use the identical inspection method. In fact, the inspection method is a key element of any specified attribute.

To demonstrate the potential large and negative fiscal consequences of failing to agree upon the inspection method for a specified characteristic, consider the case of a manufacturer of expensive chemical reactors made from 316L stainless steel. This stainless steel consists chemically of approximately 69 percent iron, 17 percent chromium, 12 percent nickel, 2 percent molybdenum, and a trace of carbon. When the manufacturer receives a shipment of 316L stainless steel from the supplier, a number of physical tests, such as tensile strength, will be performed to determine adherence to the respective physical specifications. In addition, the chemical composition will probably be checked. Assume that the reactor manufacturer and the 316L stainless steel supplier have agreed to a percentage of nickel specification of 11.75 to 12.25 percent. The supplier agrees that he or she can control the nickel to within these limits. The producer agrees that he or she can manufacture acceptable reactors if the nickel is controlled within these limits. However, the two parties forget to specify the method to be used to measure the nickel content. The stainless steel supplier uses method A to be certain that the product is suitable for shipment to the customer. The reactor producer uses method B to ensure that the stainless steel receipts are acceptable for use.

During the first year of production, all stainless steel deliveries meet the nickel specification. However, the supplier's method A gave an average nickel content of 11.97 percent, whereas the producer's method B *gave an average of 11.85 percent nickel. Since no out-of-specification situations occurred, no one is overly concerned or possibly has even noticed that method B* is yielding significantly lower results than method *A*. Then, the supplier ships a load of stainless steel valued at $500,000. His or her analytical results gave a nickel content of 11.80 percent. The reactor producer's analytical result, however, is 11.70 percent, demonstrating the same bias relative to the supplier's result that had been occurring all along. The reactor producer wants to reject this shipment because it does not comply with the specification, but the supplier maintains that the stainless steel does comply with the specification. It may be very difficult to resolve the question: which method gives the correct result? In addition, the reactor producer probably used results from method *B* to agree originally to the nickel specification on the basis that acceptable reactors could be produced with nickel contents between 11.75 and 12.25 percent. Because the two parties forgot to specify the method to be used for checking the nickel content of the stainless steel, a substantial amount of money is at stake. Furthermore, the good working relationship between the supplier and the customer may be at stake.

In the above example, if the same bias existed while the two parties were using the same test method, the situation could have been readily resolved. When a single method is used, there can be only one accurate result. This can be closely approximated by performing a sufficient number of analyses so that the statistical variation associated with the mean approaches zero. Therefore, in this situation, both the supplier and the producer could agree to abide by the average result from an independent laboratory based on an appropriate number of samples and analyses. Both parties would, of course, have to affirm that the independent laboratory was indeed performing the test properly. However, when different methods are used, it is entirely feasible that a real bias exists between the test methods.

Source of Supply

In many cases, it is necessary to specify that the component supplier *maintain a constant source of supply for the materials used to produce or to supply the component.* For example, flavor is probably the most important attribute to consumers of tomato juice. Since the flavor of the juice depends on the species of tomato and on the environment in which it is grown, tomato juice producers (if they do not cultivate their own supply) should specify that their tomato suppliers ship them only the desired tomato species and that they be grown in particular locations.

Manufacturing Process

Another factor which is usually desirable to specify is that the *supplier utilize a constant manufacturing process for producing the component.* The supplier should not make a process change without informing the customer of the plan before the change is actually made.

As an illustration of how a seemingly minor process change for a component can cause a significant alteration in a final product, consider the marketer of a liquid, water white rug cleaner. Assume that the detergent component for this product is made in solid form. The detergent supplier uses a chemical reactor to produce the substance in solution and drying equipment to concentrate the detergent into its solid form. Subsequent to the drying operation, the detergent is air blown through stainless steel piping into drums. The drumming operation is sufficiently slow that it limits the production rate of this detergent. When the detergent maker's sales personnel consummate a contract with a new customer, the drumming bottleneck must be eliminated so that the additional business can be accomodated. To do this, the detergent supplier installs a second drumming station using copper piping which happens to be available. Should the producer of the rug cleaner be informed of this apparently harmless change which doesn't even involve the major equipment used for reacting and drying? If the rug cleaner were colored blue, it probably wouldn't matter. However, this change could have a significant effect on a water white rug cleaner. If this detergent abrades the copper piping such that even relatively small quantities of copper impurities enter the detergent, the water white product could very well take on a bluish discoloration. This is because many detergents contain excess sulfates. When copper and sulfate are together in a water base, as when the solid detergent is dissolved in water to produce the rug cleaner, the mixture usually becomes bluish.

Packaging

Another factor which must be considered relative to Component Specifications is *how the component should be packaged in order to be adequately protected prior to use*. Many of the paper labels used for a multitude of consumer products, like applesauce in jars, tend to curl when exposed to high humidity conditions. This makes it very difficult for users to affix the labels in the correct position to their packages. This problem can be avoided by specifying that labels be packaged in a plastic film resistant to moisture, prior to storage and shipment. As another example, a bottler of a high-grade, liquid chemical reagent should specify that his or her bottle supplier position all empty bottles upside down in their boxes to minimize the possibility of foreign material entering the bottles during storage and shipment.

Storage and Shipping Conditions

In some cases, specification of how the component is packaged is not sufficient to adequately protect the component from its environment. For this situation, *storage and shipping conditions at and from the supplier's location must also be specified*. These conditions can include temperature, humidity, amount of light, and length of time stored.

To illustrate, take the case of an ice cream manufacturer who obtains artificial flavors from a supplier located in the southwestern United States. Many flavors begin to deteriorate chemically at temperatures over approximately 80°F. Therefore, to ensure that customers experience flavor satisfaction, the ice cream manufacturer should specify that the flavors be stored and shipped at temperatures below 80°F. In the Southwest, this specification could require air conditioning and shipment in refrigerated vehicles. In addition, to a much lesser extent, some degradation of flavors can occur even at 70°F. To prevent this from becoming a problem, the ice cream manufacturer should specify the length of time that the flavors can be stored at the supplier's location prior to shipment. Obviously, the ice cream manufacturer will also have to control the storage temperature and time at the company's own site.

A different type of example occurs when bulk liquids must be transported from supplier to customer. It is wise for the customer to specify that the vehicles used to transfer the bulk liquid be thoroughly cleaned and inspected prior to use. Imagine milk being filled into a tank truck which just previously had transported castor oil! Situations like this do occur.

An Illustration of the Importance of Well-Designed Component Specifications

The following scenario, which I encountered a number of years ago, highlights the importance of allocating sufficient and well-qualified personnel resources to design comprehensive Component Specifications. The product involved was an opaque, yellow car wax with the consistency of a paste and was sold principally in cans containing 120 grams of product. It had been nationally marketed for about 4 years when this incident took place. As the product was filled into the cans, it had a very low viscosity, almost like water. However, as the product set in the warehouse, it "firmed up" to the desired paste viscosity. This firming-up process normally required about 10 days. For this reason, and because product consistency was an important attribute to product users, standard operating procedure required that all production segments be held in the warehouse for a minimum of 14 days so that a delayed inspection could be performed at 10 to 14 days after production. This was to ensure that the relevant production had in fact firmed up to the desired extent.

On a particular day in January when the inspector was routinely checking a sample of 14-day-old product for the reason mentioned above, she was startled to discover that approximately 20 percent of the cans contained product with one to three circular purple spots about 3 millimeters in diameter on the surface of the product. Further investigation divulged that all production between 11 and 14 days old manifested the same phenomenon. Product less than 11 days old demonstrated the same spots, but the incidence level diminished toward zero as the age of the product progressed downward toward 6 days old. Product younger than 6 days old exhibited normal surface characteristics. The spots were not evident in any sample for product below the top surface. Previous testing had disclosed that iron in the presence of oxygen could react with one of the formula ingredients of this product resulting in a purple-colored compound. It was known that this reaction would only proceed to a noticeable degree if the iron was present in the product at a concentration of 50 parts per million (ppm) or greater. It was precisely for this reason that all Component Specifications relating to this product included an "iron content" requirement of "10 ppm or less".

Initially it was thought that perhaps an error had occurred and that one of the component ingredients did indeed contain an excessive quantity of iron or that the additive effect from all component ingredients exceeded the 50-ppm limit. A review of the results from analytical tests conducted when the ingredients were received revealed that only the major liquid ingredient of the recipe possessed any measurable amount of iron, and that this level was only 6 ppm. Thinking that possibly a nonrepresentative sample may have been obtained for one of the components, all ingredients were resampled and rechecked for iron. The new results merely confirmed the original ones.

At this point, it was suspected that the source of the iron, if in fact iron was causing the problem, must be from within the manufacturing system for the product. Both the processing and packaging operations were halted. All equipment was washed out and disassembled to the greatest extent possible. However, a detailed examination of the system was unable to uncover even a remote location where iron might be entering the product. Simultaneous with these activities, sophisticated analytical chemical techniques confirmed that the circular purple spots had been caused by iron reacting with an ingredient in the presence of oxygen. These purple spots presented both potential aesthetic and safety concerns. However, the safety concern was speedily alleviated when several references clearly demonstrated that the (purple) compound had been thoroughly tested and was not in any way hazardous. On the other hand, the possibility of product users not being aware of this and reacting quite unfavorably remained a worrisome subject.

The above activities had already consumed 4 working days during which time, for obvious reasons, no additional production occurred. During this time, further warehoused product which had progressed to then be 11 to 14 days old also manifested approximately 20 percent incidence level of the "measles." Product less than 6 days old when the product was initially discovered, and which was now greater than 6 days old, also showed purple spots. During this period, it was also determined that for production which had a penchant for acquiring the "measles" in 11 to 14 days in the warehouse, the same phenomenon could be accelerated by placing production at 140°F for 24 hours. In other words, the 140°F, 24-hour test provided an excellent means of predicting what would actually occur within 11 to 14 days for warehoused product. Consequently, the decision was made to reassemble all equipment, thoroughly clean it, and produce product for an additional day. Production from various times during that day would be subjected to the 24-hour predictive test. Obviously, the hope was that the source of the "measles" would have "gone away."

However, as is normally the situation, problems do not disappear without positive and effective actions being invoked. This was no exception. The source of the "measles" was indeed still present. By this time 11 working days of double-shift production had been generated with all of it containing about a 20 percent incidence level of circular, purple spots, and 4 days, or 8 shifts, of production had been lost. At this point, a high-level decision was announced that no additional production would be initiated until the problem source was identified and corrected. The investigative effort was heavily reinstituted. Another 3 working days and a weekend passed with nothing but frustrations to show. By this time, the 11 days of production had yielded 1,336,550 cans of product with a total value of $307,407. (This is the result of the packaging operation running at 150 units per minute, two shifts per day for 11 days, and with a 90 percent efficiency.) Furthermore, 7 production days had been lost. In net, 18 consecutive production days had passed without any pro²uction segment suitable for shipment. Many product obligations to retail outlets were unable to be honored. This meant that some stores were beginning to exhaust their stock of the product, thereby giving previously loyal product users no choice but to switch brands. Consumer actions of this kind may be difficult to quantify in monetary terms, but, as we shall clearly see in Part III, they can be highly detrimental to the profits of a business.

One evening, four exhausted people were present in the plant laboratory commiserating another day of failure to solve the "measles" problem and halfheartedly examining samples of the components used to produce the last product batch. One person ran his hand through the sample jar of the major liquid component. When he withdrew his hand two tiny metallic particles were evident on the end of a finger. At once activity and conversation increased immensely. Within 30 minutes, the source of the problem had been correctly identified, although another 36 hours were required in order to confirm the solution. Recall that analytical results had demonstrated that this major liquid component contained iron at 6 ppm which would not have been deleterious to the product. This was true. Following the prescribed test method, the laboratory had accurately determined that a 1000-gram sample of this liquid did contain 0.006 grams of iron, which is 6 ppm of iron. However, when the iron is present in solid form, there are 0 ppm iron in the liquid, but the solid particles consist of 1,000,000 ppm, or 100 percent, of iron. That is, every iron particle contacted the product with a concentration of 1,000,000 ppm of iron, highly in excess of the 50 ppm concentration needed for the deleterious reaction to occur. As stated earlier, in order to take place, this reaction also required oxygen. This is the reason it was evident only on surfaces exposed to the atmosphere and not in bulk product.

In retrospect, what had actually happened follows. Unbeknownst to the vendor of the major liquid component, a significant corrosion problem for this material had started to occur at his manufacturing facility. The corrosion resulted in iron particles of approximately 100-micron (0.1 millimeter) diameter accumulating in the liquid at an average concentration of 3 iron particles per 2 grams of the liquid. Since this liquid constituted about 33 percent of the product, on the average, each 2 grams of product contained 1 iron particle. Although the vendor of the liquid required a substantial amount of time to locate and rectify the problem, manufacturing of the product was able to resume after the installation of a 50-micron filter between the storage tank for the liquid and the mixing tank for the product. This filter retention capability was sufficient to eliminate the smallest of the iron particles from the liquid stream without sacrificing its addition rate.

The epilogue to the "measles enigma" was that a new preventive item was added to the Component Specification: "particulate iron—none present." As an added safeguard, the liquid filter was left in place. In the aftermath of this incident, a fortuitous circumstance occurred. It turned out that at about 1 month after the manufacture of production exhibiting purple spots (about 2 to 3 weeks after the spots appeared), these purple spots miraculously vanished. The purplish iron compound had diffused into the bulk product thereby diluting the discolored portion to the extent that the normal color returned. All of the $307,407 worth of questionable product became recoverable. However, the monetary loss owing to being unable to deliver product to retail customers during the problem time frame remained unknown, but almost certainly it was a significant loss. In summary, the scenario described here was due entirely to a nuance of a Component Specification. This should be sufficient testimony to the importance of well-designed and comprehensive Component Specifications.

Summary

For each and every component used to manufacture a product, there are certain factors which must be considered to determine the appropriate characteristics that need to be included in the Component Specification. These factors are:

1. Requirements for functional, aesthetic, safety, sanitation, and regulatory attributes and the respective limits

2. The inspection method to be used for each specified characteristic

3. The source of materials used to make or supply the component

4. A constant process for getting the component into the desired form

5. Packaging requirements

6. Storage and shipping conditions at and from the supplier's location.

THE SUPPLIER QUALIFICATION PROGRAM

A Component Specification is developed for a component by considering all of the factors covered in the above discussion. The resulting Component Specification defines all the limits and respective inspection methods which are important in order for receipts of that component to be routinely acceptable for use. A supplier(s) must be found who can and will meet the Specification. This is accomplished via a supplier qualification program with an objective of obtaining a competent and ethical supplier. Obviously, this objective must be accomplished for each and every component.

Past Performance Assessment

The first factor that must be considered in qualifying potential suppliers is an *evaluation of the firm's past performance*. In many cases, the suppliers have been producing the desired component for other customers for a substantial period of time. For this situation, a thorough review of the potential suppliers' data can provide a good assessment of their ability to meet the quality requirements. In cases in which the component has not been previously manufactured by the potential suppliers, a review of their overall quality record can provide valuable information. This review should include a determination of the frequency at which customers reject shipments of their components. A firm's quality reputation throughout the industry can also be a useful indicator of a potential supplier's quality capability. Regardless of how it is accomplished, a customer must be convinced that a potential supplier's past quality record is consistent with the customer's requirements.

Facilities and Personnel Evaluation

An evaluation of the potential supplier's facilities and personnel should be made. While touring the prospective supplier's manufacturing facility for the component, at least the following should be achieved:

1. Obtain a basic understanding of the relevant production operation. This will provide a base from which to monitor for process changes. Also, it can provide input as to the necessity for additional items to be specified in the Component Specification. If the potential supplier uses a chromium-lined reactor to produce a chemical, it might be desirable to add an item regarding the concentration of chromium permitted in the chemical.

2. Assess the probability of errors occurring in the operation. For example, during the production of chemical component A, how likely is it that chemical B produced in an immediately adjacent area could be mislabeled as A?

3. Determine if adequate laboratory, utility, warehouse, and other auxiliary facilities are available to support the operation.

4. Ascertain that sufficient manufacturing capacity is available to cover present and anticipated needs.

5. Make an overall judgment regarding the capability of the operation to routinely produce acceptable component on a continuing basis.

When evaluating potential suppliers' personnel, the two key elements to look for are technical competence and ethical behavior. Technical competence greatly increases the probability that suppliers will emphasize the prevention of quality problems before they occur and can rapidly solve problems if they do happen. It is essential that suppliers conduct their operations in a professional and ethical manner. Suppliers' operations cannot, and should not have to be, monitored continuously. Therefore, their commitments and their communciations must be reliable.

Sample Evaluation

At this point, the details of the Component Specification should be discussed so that the prospective supplier clearly understands the customer's specific requirements. The next step in the qualification program is the *evaluation of samples of the component submitted by the supplier*. The evaluation is twofold: an evaluation of the component sample versus all items specified in the Component Specification; and an evaluation of product made utilizing the sample component. This can range from a very simple to an extremely complex and time-consuming procedure, depending upon the component and the product.

To illustrate, consider buttons to be used in the manufacture of men's suits. Upon receiving a sample from the potential supplier, the suit manufacturer can readily inspect the buttons versus the respective specifications for color, dimensions, strength, and so on. Then, some buttons can be sewn onto suits to ensure that no problems occur in attaching them and that their appearance on the suits is acceptable.

Contrast this simple procedure with that necessary for a new chemical to be incorporated as the active ingredient in a drug to treat high blood pressure. For this case, the prospective supplier will probably elect not to invest capital in a production facility until, via a contract, he or she is certain of having a market for the component. Consequently, the initial sample will probably have been produced in a laboratory or pilot plant facility. After the drug producer checks the respective specifications, a batch (or more) of the drug will be made using the sample of the active ingredient. The batch will be tested against product specifications. Testing will be necessary to ensure that the product using the component is safe and effective for human use. Testing of aged product will be necessary to ensure the retention of effectiveness and safety after exposure to environmental conditions similar to what will be encountered through its expected lifetime. A year or more may be required to complete all of this and other testing. Then the drug manufacturer is ready to commit contractually to the supplier, and consequently the supplier is prepared to invest capital in a production facility for the chemical. Significant time may be required to construct and start up the facility. When a sample is available from the production facility, sample and product evaluations may need to be repeated to prove that this material is the same as that produced using the pilot plant equipment. Obviously, this entire procedure can be a very lengthy one.

Consider the following situation regarding a rather well-advertised after shave lotion. Among other formula components, this product contains glycerine and a fragrance. The fragrance represents a very important attribute for a product of this nature. Fragrances commonly consist of a variety of chemical species which tend to react chemically with many other substances. When this takes place, the nature of the fragrance can be substantially altered, usually in an undesirable manner. It is mainly for this reason that products containing fragrances must be thoroughly tested for product aging characteristics. This testing must be conducted using the specific components which will be employed in the formula.

Glycerine can be derived either from naturally occuring fats and oils or synthetically from propylene via a number of different chemical processes. Significantly different chemicals are used for these processes. Although in all cases the glycerine is subsequently purified, normally it will not attain a purity of 100 percent. Consequently, trace remnants of whatever chemicals are used in the process may be present in the glycerine. In many situations, these minor differences are benign for all practical purposes. In the case of the after shave lotion, naturally derived glycerine from one properly qualified vendor had been successfully used for years. Then, in 1980, the reliable supplier experienced a temporary difficulty in meeting the component specification for color. To obviate the tight glycerine inventory situation which ensued, a supply of glycerine was ordered from a different vendor who claimed that his synthetically produced glycerine could meet all of the Component Specification requirements. In fact, it did. Production continued for about two weeks with this glycerine until the original supplier's quality problem was alleviated. All of the after shave lotion made with the synthetically derived glycerine adhered to its Finished Product Specification.

About four months later, a burgeoning wave of complaints started to be received regarding the odor of the after shave lotion. Many of the complaints were vehement, describing the malodor as putrid, vile, or rotten. A significant number alleged that they would not repurchase the brand. Detective work revealed that every one of these complaints was related to the product made from synthetic glycerine. Subsequent testing utilizing retained samples of natural and synthetic glycerine conclusively proved that the malodor was indeed the result of a slow reaction between an ingredient of the fragrance and one of the by-product impurities in the synthetic glycerine. A properly conducted, professional qualification program for the vendor of the synthetic glycerine would probably have prevented the profit loss which was experienced. With a little foresight to realize that an alternate glycerine supplier might one day be a valuable asset, such a qualification program could have been completed.

Component Variability Evaluation

The next factor that must be assessed is the *quality variability of the component*. This can be done by evaluating finished product made using samples from different supplier production lots of the component. The variability which can be expected during actual production can be more closely approximated when these samples are obtained at different times from the supplier. This increases the probability of evaluating component samples representing the maximum variability and of assessing the sometimes important variable of the season of the year. The latter is especially important if temperature and/or humidity fluctuations can affect the component.

Written Agreement

Assuming favorable results for a given supplier's component relative to all of the previously discussed factors in the supplier qualification program, the customer is now prepared to consummate the qualification of this vendor. The most important factor in the supplier qualification program is to *obtain the supplier's written agreement that he or she can and will comply with all the items included in the Component Specification*. Without this agreement all other measures taken to control component quality are academic. It is important that the Component Specification again be discussed attribute by attribute with the prospective vendor to ensure that the requirements are thoroughly comprehended. Only then can the supplier knowledgeably agree that he or she can routinely deliver shipments of components which comply with all specifications. The supplier must also agree that for shipments which do not conform with specifications, either the nonconformity will be corrected or return of the shipment will be accepted. On the other hand, the customer agrees to accept and pay for all component shipments ordered which conform to the Component Specification. By inference, the customer is agreeing that with these components product can be manufactured which meets the finished product specifications. This mutual agreement concludes the qualification of one supplier for a particular component.

Multiple Qualified Suppliers

It is wise to *consider the benefits of qualifying at least two suppliers for each component*. When a producer has only one qualified supplier for a component, an increased risk regarding component price, availability, and quality is being assumed. From a quality perspective, if the supplier experiences a quality problem which requires significant time to identify and/or correct, the manufacturer may consume the supply of acceptable component before an additional quantity becomes available. In this situation, the producer is faced with the "no-win" decision of either using substandard component to produce substandard product, or of not producing and thereby giving customers the opportunity to purchase another brand or product. In either case, the direct effect is a decrease in profits for the producer. The existence of a second qualified supplier can avoid this no-win situation. This subject is discussed further in Chapter 5 in the context of inventory control.

Surveillance Program

Finally, a supplier visit program should be implemented. The purpose of the program is to maintain open communications with the supplier so that potential trouble areas can be corrected before they become real problems, and to check the supplier's facilities and personnel at some frequency to ascertain if significant changes have occurred. The frequency of these visits to a particular supplier depends mainly on his or her quality performance, how critical the component is to the producer, and the number of qualified alternate suppliers.

Summary

To obtain competent and ethical component suppliers a Supplier Qualification Program should be utilized. For each potential component supplier this program involves an assessment of past quality record; facilities and personnel; sample(s) of the component including product made using the sample; and the degree of component variability likely to be experienced. If these results are favorable, and if the supplier agrees in writing to meet the terms of the Component Specification, he or she should be designated as qualified to supply a certain component. In order to minimize the risk of poor-quality components interrupting production, it is wise to qualify at least two suppliers for each component and to maintain a supplier visit program.

4 The Recipe

The recipe is the specification of the quantity of each component which is needed to manufacture a specific amount of a given product. Many products are produced by combining a number of chemical components into a homogeneous liquid or solid. Colognes, body powders, toothpastes, paints, and drummed liquid chemical products are examples. For this type of product, two recipes are commonly employed: (a) for combining the chemical components into the homogeneous product, and (b) for the assembly of the homogeneous product into its final, packaged form ready for shipment to the trade. An example of the first kind of recipe (for a brushless shaving cream product) is presented in Table 4-1.

Many other products, such as television sets, automobiles, dining room tables, refrigerators, and lawn mowers are produced via assembly operations. An example of a recipe for an assembly operation to produce a chess game is shown in Table 4-2. This type of recipe is analogous to the type of recipe which would be used for the packaging operation described in (b) above. For the chess game and for the brushless shave cream, typical finished product specifications are also presented to facilitate the discussion which follows.

DESIGN

Support from Component Specifications and Vendor Qualifications

When designing a recipe, one very important factor to consider is that *every component included in the recipe should be supported by an appropriate Component Specification and a listing of the vendors who have been qualified to furnish the part or substance*. The importance of these topics was covered in the previous chapter. In addition, each component should be identified in such a way that absolutely no doubt exists as to the applicable Com-

**TABLE 4-1.   Example of a Recipe and Finished Product Specification
for a Typical Brushless Shaving Cream**

RECIPE	
Component	Quantity
Glycerol monostearate (CS No. 5)	1100 pounds
Lanolin (CS No. 237)	400 pounds
Sorbitol (CS No. 55)	300 pounds
Sodium stearate (CS No. 75)	200 pounds
Mineral oil (CS No. 642)	200 pounds
Proprietary fragrance (CS No. 27)	10 pounds
Blue dye (CS No. 15)	4–5 pounds[a]
Methyl cellulose (CS No. 39)	30–45 pounds[b]
Water (CS No. 1)	Sufficient to yield 10,000 total pounds of product

FINISHED PRODUCT SPECIFICATION		
Attribute	Specification	Test Method
Glycerol monostearate (%)	10.8%–11.2%	A
Product consistency at 70ºF	4 mm–8 mm penetration	B
Product odor	No detectable difference when compared to standard sample	C
Product color	No noticeable difference when compared to standard sample	D
Product appearance	Free of foreign material; smooth texture	E
Bacteria testing	No colonies detected	F

[a] Adjust usage as necessary within the range shown so as to meet the FPS color limit.
[b] Adjust usage as necessary within the range shown so as to meet the FPS consistency limits.

ponent Specification and list of qualified vendors. To illustrate, suppose the producer of the chess game referred to in Table 4-2 also produces a deluxe, more expensive one with a larger playing board and larger chess pieces. If the recipe for the regular model in Table 4-2 merely identified the components as kings, bishops, or pawns, the purchaser could easily obtain a game which contained some pieces from the deluxe game and some pieces from the standard game. However, if the pieces are identified in the recipe in a manner similar to that demonstrated in Tables 4-1 and 4-2 with concrete references to the pertinent component specifications, there should be no question as to the size and color of the pieces required in any one box.

Accuracy Requirement

Another important factor is the *accuracy implied by the recipe*. For example, most consumers are attuned to the odor of the products they buy. The recipe shown in Table 4-1 for a typical shaving cream includes the use of 10 pounds of a proprietary fragrance. Expressing the weight of the fragrance, or any other component, in this manner infers that any

TABLE 4-2. Example of a Recipe and Finished Product Specification for a Chess Game

RECIPE	
Component	Quantity
King per CS No. 131	1
King per CS No. 132	1
Queen per CS No. 133	1
Queen per CS No. 134	1
Rooks per CS No. 135	2
Rooks per CS No. 136	2
Bishops per CS No. 137	2
Bishops per CS No. 138	2
Knights per CS No. 139	2
Knights per CS No. 140	2
Pawns per CS No. 141	8
Pawns per CS No. 142	8
Playing board per CS No. 154	1
Playing instructions per CS No. 155	1
Box per CS No. 156	1

FINISHED PRODUCT SPECIFICATION

Attribute	Specification	Test method
Product components	All pieces designated in the recipe are present	A
Product assembly	All components wrapped as per diagram in test method	B
Manufacturing code	Must be legible on bottom of box and show month/day/year of production	C
Product condition	No visible marks or scratches on any component; all printed copy on box and game instructions legible	D

weight between 9.50 and 10.49 pounds is acceptable. (Any weight in this range rounded off to the nearest whole number—as in the recipe—will yield 10 pounds.) This means that any two batches of the shaving cream could differ in the amount of perfume added by as much as 10 percent. For many situations, a variation even of this magnitude may not be discernible to consumers, even as the product ages. However, in many other situations, this amount of variability might be readily detectable by and objectionable to users of the product. The more delicate the fragrance, as in an expensive women's perfume, the more likely this will be a potential problem. Consider that a simple change in the manner of stating the weight of this fragrance to be used in a 10,000-pound batch of the shaving cream from 10 pounds to 10.0 pounds would restrict the range of additions from 9.950 to 10.049 pounds, or to 1 percent, a tenfold reduction in the amount of variation which is permitted. The point is that in the preparation of any product recipe, the potential consequence of expressing component quantification in the intended manner should be studied.

Practical for Manufacturing

The prototype of a product manifests the product's degree of excellence. By definition, the prototype recipe consists of a fixed amount of a single vendor shipment of each component that is included in the product. This *recipe must subsequently be translated into a practical manufacturing recipe without compromising the product's degree of excellence*. This means that the manufacturing recipe must be developed in conjunction with all Component Specifications, the Finished Product Specification, operating procedures, and equipment capabilities so that for the spectrum of circumstances which can occur, the FPS can be adhered to. The margarine example presented in Chapter 2, in the context of "overall design," demonstrated the need to manage this factor.

As an illustration of a pragmatic recipe for a manufacturing operation, refer again to the recipe in Table 4-1 for a 10,000-pound batch of shaving cream. Note that for the blue dye and for the methyl cellulose used to thicken the product, weight usage is expressed as a range rather than as a fixed amount. This is because, even in today's highly technical world, many chemicals which exhibit complex molecular structures, such as dyes and cellulosic or other polymeric materials, cannot be produced without batch-to-batch nuances. It is not highly unusual to find that the usage of fixed amounts of these materials does not always allow the relevant product specifications to be met. When for any reason it is not possible to liberalize these product specifications, consideration should be given to permitting usage of the component within a defined range. The range is usually determined empirically by making product which incorporates different receipts (component lots) of the particular component in question and a variety of receipts of the other components in the recipe. When a component usage range is adopted, it is normally also judicious to test products representing the entire range to ensure that their aging patterns are similar.

Summary

The important factors to be considered while developing a product recipe are that every component in the recipe be buttressed by a Component Specification and a list of qualified suppliers, that the accuracy implicit in the way component quantity is specified suits the accuracy needed, and that it will be practical for a manufacturing operation.

5 Manufacturing Operations

After Component Specifications have been developed and after suitable suppliers have been qualified, the producer must be able to routinely combine the components received so that the finished product will possess the desired characteristics. This is accomplished by the heart of a producer's business, manufacturing. Beginning with the receiving of components from suppliers, manufacturing includes all operations and related activities which are utilized in order to deliver finished product containing these components to customers. In this chapter, we shall discuss the multitude of factors which must be examined to determine proper actions so that quality goals can be achieved for the overall manufacturing process.

PREVENTING FAILURE COSTS DURING COMPONENT AND PRODUCT HANDLING

A qualified vendor's responsibility for guaranteeing that a component shipment complies with its Component Specification usually ceases when the shipment is accepted at the user's manufacturing site. Thus, to avoid failure costs, a manufacturer must ascertain that component shipments are actually acceptable as received and must protect them from abnormal physical and chemical deterioration from the time of acceptance to the time of use. Similarly, a manufacturer must maintain acceptable finished product in that condition from the time manufacturing is completed at least until the time it is delivered to customers and must be certain that only acceptable product is shipped to customers. To ensure that these desirable actions do happen, a manufacturer should institute appropriate preventive and appraisal measures relating to each of the factors covered in this chapter's next two sections: "Preventing Failure Costs for the Entire Manufacturing Process" and "Prevention and Appraisal Measures as Insurance Against Unexpected Failure Costs," which pertain to the total manufacturing operation.

Some of the factors which need to be considered for preventive measures are limited in relevance to mainly the component and product handling portion of manufacturing operations, and they constitute the topic for this section of the chapter. However, it should be noted that although the following discussion is in the context of components and finished product, the same factors should also be considered for any circumstance where material is accumulated and stored for a significant time period. For example, these factors should be examined if an inventory of partially completed product is maintained.

Release System

A very important factor to consider is *the procedure by which components are routinely released for use in manufacturing* and *the procedure by which finished product is routinely released for shipment to the customer.* A "released" designation for components denotes that the represented components can be used to produce product. Similarly, a "released" designation for finished goods denotes that the represented product can be shipped to customers.

Release systems can range from rigidly positive to completely negative. The selection of a system for a given situation depends mainly upon the potential consequences if unacceptable components are erroneously used in manufacturing or if unacceptable product is mistakenly shipped to customers. Simply stated, a rigid positive release system mandates that any specific quantity of components or product cannot be used or shipped, respectively, until an officially designated person gives written authorization for that action. This authorization will be granted based on favorable results relative to a previously agreed-upon criterion. The criterion usually involves confirmation via some established sampling plan that the component receipt adheres to its Component Specification or that the production segment adheres to its Finished Product Specification. Often this release will only be valid for a definite time period. If component use or product shipment has not occurred when that time expires, the release must be reestablished. This procedure is especially useful when the potential for a significant degree of component or product deterioration is known to exist.

In the strictest application, released and unreleased materials are separated by physical barriers. This type of system is commonly employed for the production of pharmaceuticals. In this industry, if a segment of production shipped to the trade does not meet product specifications, the safety and well-being of the humans who use it may be risked. In addition, if it is discovered after the fact, the cost to recall and salvage or scrap the product can be enormous. Furthermore, very substantial intangible costs can be incurred from the negative publicity associated with a product recall.

A totally negative release system allows any components to be used or any product to be shipped at any time, unless a reason happens to be found for not doing so before the action has taken place. In other words, components are automatically released for use upon receipt, and product is automatically released for shipment as soon as it is produced. This situation could exist in the production of relatively simple products like paper clips. The producer might elect to ship paper clips whenever they are needed even if testing has not been completed, because the risk is judged to be negligible that any amount of production will be unfit for use. The point of this discussion is simply that failure to fully assess the type of release system which is needed for a specific application can result in high failure costs.

Responsibility For Determining Disposition of Subquality Material

A second factor is the *establishment of responsibility for determining the disposition of a component receipt or production segment which does not meet the relevant specification.* It is virtually impossible to have a standard operating procedure for this situation because of the infinite number of possibilities which exist, and because each occurrence usually needs to be considered relative to the circumstances existing at that time. The responsibility for a decision of this nature should reside with a person or group with both the technical competence and business acumen to capably evaluate the options available. For a component receipt the choices are basically: reject the shipment; alleviate the deficiency (e.g., inspecting a shipment of bottle caps to remove two percent which are cracked); or use it as is. For a segment of production, the choices are generally to scrap, which is costly; to salvage, if feasible, to render the production acceptable (e.g., inspect out the defective units or blend bulk product at low concentration into new batches); or to ship as is. If consumer safety is a risk, shipping as is is not an option. Otherwise the alternative selected will be the one associated with the least failure cost. The failure cost analysis must include an estimate of lost future sales owing to consumer dissatisfaction with the nonconforming product. In Part III, it will be demonstrated that lost sales can constitute a large monetary value.

As an example of determining the disposition of out-of-specifications material, take the case of a baseball bat manufacturer. Suppose a shipment of lumber arrives which is intended for making bats for certain major league players. However, it is determined that the lumber is too soft to conform with the hardness specification for these products. Assume that the lumber is sufficiently hard to conform with the bat manufacturer's specification for little league bats. The bat producer might decide, if the lumber supplier will agree, to dispose of the lumber by accepting it at a reduced price and using it to manufacture completely acceptable little league bats. However, a person or a group in the baseball bat producer's organization needs to be designated as the final authority to make a decision of this type. Otherwise, resolution may remain in limbo. When this happens, the possibility increases for the component or product to be erroneously used or shipped, or it can deteriorate to the point of being unsalvageable.

Inventory Control

Inventory Control is not exclusively a quality responsibility, but it can have a profound effect upon quality. *By inventory control we mean the quantity of component on hand which has been released as fit for use*, or *the quantity of product in storage which has been released as suitable for shipment to the market*. Stated differently, this includes only component *known* to be useable and product *known* to be shippable. With a negative release system, this includes all components and all product on hand. Inventory control is important to product quality in order to avoid the kind of no-win decision previously discussed in the context of the benefits of having more than one qualified supplier for each component. For any component, both inventory control and having at least two qualified suppliers must be considered to prevent the no-win choice of whether to produce substandard product or no product.

To illustrate, assume that an automobile assembly operation receives a shipment of speedometers every Monday to support automobile production for that week. This means that the supply of speedometers will be exhausted at the conclusion of each week. Assume, further, that only one qualified supplier is available for this component and that 1 week is consumed between the time an order is placed and the time when the speedometer shipment is delivered to the automobile plant. If a shipment of speedometers arrives which does not conform with its Component Specification, the automobile assembler cannot obtain a substitute shipment for a full week. Therefore, he or she must decide between the disadvantages of producing cars with substandard speedometers and the disadvantages of producing no cars at all during that week. If the speedometer defect involves a safety risk to the consumer, only the latter option exists. If the speedometer supplier cannot identify or correct the cause of the defect immediately, the situation will persist.

Even if an alternate qualified supplier had been available, the situation would not have been significantly changed, unless the alternate supplier could make a very rapid delivery on short notice. The second supplier would, however, decrease the probability that the no-win decision would perpetuate beyond 1 week. It is unlikely that a second qualified supplier would simultaneously be producing defective speedometers. However, had the automobile assembler maintained a 1-week or more minimum inventory level of released speedometers, car production could have proceeded normally while a replacement shipment was obtained. The minimum inventory level which can be tolerated for a component should be determined based on the lead time required from order until receipt, the probability of obtaining a substitute receipt which will be acceptable for use, and the extent to which the component can deteriorate during storage.

The situation for finished product is very analagous to that for components. A producer should maintain an adequate inventory of released product so that if a quality problem arises, he or she can continue to fulfill customer needs without having to decide whether to ship substandard product or to disappoint the customer with no product. The minimum inventory level for finished product should be determined based on anticipated customer needs, an assessment of the time required to correct most problems likely to occur, and the extent to which the product can deteriorate during storage.

The reader should keep in mind that the above discussion for both components and product is strictly from a product quality perspective. There are other considerations, such as the cost of maintaining a given inventory level and protection against a disaster like a fire or an earthquake, which can have a strong impact upon the decision as to the minimum inventory level to be maintained for a particular component or product.

The factors discussed so far in this chapter relate to avoiding failure costs due to the use of unacceptable components or due to the shipment of unacceptable product. The remaining factors in this section relate to maintaining acceptable components and acceptable finished product in acceptable condition to the time of use and customer delivery, respectively.

Environmental Conditions

An obvious factor to be considered is the *effect of environmental conditions.* We have previously discussed that many flavor materials can begin to undergo significant chemical deterioration at temperatures above 80°F. Therefore, an ice cream producer will probably include in the Component Specification for an artificial flavor an item requiring that the ingredient be shipped such that the flavor is not exposed to temperatures above 80°. In addition, the ice cream manufacturer must have adequate on-site facilities and operating procedures to prevent flavor degradation from exposure to higher temperatures.

To illustrate the situation for a finished product, consider the producer of a delicate red wine. Spoilage of wine can occur from excessive exposure to heat, light, or oxygen. Therefore, after the bottled wine has been determined to be of acceptable quality, it should be stored in a cool, dark place—a wine cellar—prior to shipment. Also, the bottles should be stored horizontally so that the cork remains moist and yields an airtight seal. Obviously, the wine producer must have facilities and operating procedures to accommodate these quality needs. In addition, provisions must be made to ensure that the wine is similarly protected when being transported from the manufacturing site to the ultimate purchaser.

Sanitation Requirements

Another factor to be considered is *the degree of sanitation* required. When the producer of a shaving cream marketed in tubes receives a shipment of empty tubes, a number of these boxes will be opened to obtain the random sample used to judge whether the particular component shipment is acceptable for use. If an operating procedure is not specified and personnel appropriately trained to adequately reseal the boxes, there is a good chance that dust, dirt, or even insects could enter some empty tubes before they are used. This operating procedure must be supported by the maintenance of a reasonably clean storage area. As an example of protecting finished product, consider the producer of breakfast cereals. To prevent attack or infestation of these products by insects and rodents during storage, a clean storage area and an effective pest control program are required. A critical criterion for the pest control program is that no chemicals be used which can affect the safety or the flavor of the cereals.

Physical Requirements

Another important factor is an evaluation of the *physical requirements* to maintain the quality integrity of components and products. For components, this might be as simple as specifying that bagged chemicals be stored off the floor, such as on pallets, so that pools of liquid cannot easily contact and be absorbed into the bags. The stacking height of product in the warehouse can be important. For example, take the case of a spray paint packaged in aerosol cans and shipped in cardboard containers of twelve cans each. As with many aerosol products, assume that the clearance between the product actuator button and the bottom of the protective plastic cover cap on the can is small. If the containers are stacked too high, the weight on top of the lower containers can be sufficient to depress the cardboard container tops and the plastic protective cover caps causing the buttons on the aerosol cans to be actuated. This will result in the product being prematurely dispensed from the can. Procedures limiting stack height, the design of stronger containers, or increasing the clearance between the cover cap and the actuator button can prevent this situation from resulting in substantial failure costs. As another product example, consider television sets packaged in heavy cardboard boxes and being transported by clamp trucks during storage and shipment. A maximum pressure setting should be specified for the system controlling the clamps in order to avoid the potential for crushing the television sets.

Effect of Surroundings

Another factor to consider is the *susceptibility of the component or product to be affected by other items in the same area*. If, in a cereal manufacturing facility, raw wheat or the finished wheat-based cereal is stored in proximity to the flavor ingredients used in other cereals, there is real potential that the wheat component and the cereal could be rendered unacceptable due to absorption of some of the volatile flavor ingredients. A textile company would not locate its warehouse downwind of any operation in the vicinity which emits waste through a stack. This avoids the potential for failure costs due to smoke absorption into the stored textile products.

First In, First Out

The *first in, first out (FIFO) principal* should be considered and usually implemented. Take the case of a producer of canned vegetable soup. Suppose that a shipment of green beans is received daily and that a 1-week inventory of these beans is maintained. If, on a given day, the beans to be used are randomly selected, their age at the time of use can range from just arrived to anything. Using this procedure it would be very difficult to control soup flavor and bean texture. Also, it is highly probable that failure costs would be significant due to some bean spoilage prior to use. On the other hand, if FIFO is employed, the producer would always be using 7-day-old beans. Assuming that the beans are adequately preserved during the 7-day period, spoilage should not occur and control of soup flavor should be more readily achieved. An almost identical situation exists from a product viewpoint for a milk processor and bottler. If FIFO is not used for milk shipments from the warehouse to customers, failure costs because of spoilage and dissatisfied consumers who experience a range of flavors among different bottles will probably be significant.

Summary

To prevent excessive quality failure costs from the improper handling of components and product, it is important that unacceptable components and product not be used or shipped, respectively; that acceptable components be maintained in acceptable condition from the time of receipt to the time of use; and that acceptable finished product be maintained in acceptable condition from production through delivery to the buyer. The factors which need to be assessed in order that adequate facilities be obtained and adequate procedures be established for these purposes are (a) the type of release system needed, (b) designation of responsibility for determining disposition of unacceptable material, (c) inventory levels, (d) the effect of environmental conditions, (e) the degree of sanitation required, (f) physical limitations, (g) potential effects from other items in proximity, and (h) FIFO.

PREVENTING FAILURE COSTS FOR THE ENTIRE MANUFACTURING PROCESS

The marketer of a product must economically provide adequate manufacturing facilities, manufacturing equipment, and define sufficient operating procedures so that for any combination of acceptable components, the finished product can adhere to product specifications. *This discussion contains the factors which need to be considered during the design of manufacturing facilities, equipment, and procedures so that preventive measures can be incorporated for avoiding excessive quality failure costs.* All phases of manufacturing are covered.

Accuracy and Precision Requirements

The first factor that needs to be considered is the *accuracy and precision of the manufacturing process*. A determination of the accuracy and precision required for the particular circumstances must be made. Then, the operation must be designed so as to comply with the requirement. Consider the accuracy needed in the weighing of ingredients to produce a new drug for the treatment of cancer contrasted with the accuracy needed to weigh ingredients for a common printer's ink for newspapers. To ensure that the cancer drug is safe and effective, it may be necessary for the producer to be certain that any weight indicated by the scale is within plus or minus 0.1 percent of the actual weight. For the newspaper ink, it may only be necessary for the producer to know that the indicated scale weight is within plus or minus 3.0 percent of the actual weight. Regardless of the actual number, the equipment and instruments used must be inherently capable of achieving whatever accuracy and precision are required for the specific use. This applies equally to laboratory and inspection equipment and instruments.

A germane part of this factor is that all equipment and instruments used must be capable of operating with the required accuracy and precision in the environmental conditions to which they will be exposed. For example, product variability can be excessive if a scale salesman quotes accuracy claims based on tests conducted at room temperature (75°F), but the scale is to be used in a room maintained at 50°F.

Another pertinent portion of this factor is that all equipment and instruments used must be capable of maintaining the required accuracy and precision for their expected lifetimes. To illustrate, suppose that a small platform scale is purchased to weigh the active ingredient for the cancer drug mentioned above. The scale company claims and can prove that their scale possesses an accuracy of plus or minus 0.1 percent of the true weight. However, product variability can go out of control if after 10 months of operation the mechanical linkages in the scale wear to the point that no matter how well the scale is calibrated, a reading within 0.1 percent of the actual weight can no longer be guaranteed.

Sanitation Requirements

A second factor is *the degree of sanitation required in the manufacturing area, for the manufacturing equipment, and for the operating personnel.* This need can range from sterility in a pharmaceutical industry application to orderly for the manufacture of pencils. For reasons related to the need for product sterility, the production of many ethical drugs is carried out in an extremely clean, totally enclosed room provided with its private source of microbially filtered air. Auxiliary equipment is present to enable a rapid and thorough cleaning and sterilization of the room and its equipment at frequent intervals. There may be a need to utilize equipment which can be readily disassembled to check the cleanliness of interior surfaces between a washout and a sterilization. When washouts and sterilizations are performed, the equipment and associated piping must be designed to allow complete drainage from the system. Operating personnel may be required to wear special, clean clothes, as well as hair and mouth coverage. These are just examples of the types of special items and procedures which may be required for this kind of operation. On the other hand, for a pencil manufacturing operation, the only real need may be for general cleanliness and orderliness to prevent the occurrence of inefficient operation and errors.

Unit Operation Design

A very important factor is the *design of each unit operation*. To assist in the prevention of failure costs, valuable quality input should be provided relating to the equipment to be utilized, the selection of conditions to be employed, and the establishment of operating procedures.

Consider the packaging of products marketed in bottles, such as pancake syrup, glue, catsup, or wine. For most bottled products, packaging includes the common basic unit operations of bottle cleaning, filling, capping, labeling, coding, and securing the bottles in shipping containers. The cleaning operation will be used to illustrate the type of quality input that can be very useful in ensuring that the equipment used is capable of preventing potential failure costs. The cleaning operation usually involves inversion of the bottles and a simultaneous, or subsequent, airblow/vacuum. The inversion is intended to remove any heavier foreign particles by gravity. The air is intended to agitate any lighter foreign particles to become airborne so that the vacuum can remove them. To determine whether a specific piece of equipment being considered for this operation can accomplish it adequately is a quality responsibility. It can be fulfilled by defining acceptance criteria based on the finished product specification pertaining to foreign material which the prospective bottle cleaner must meet. For example, the acceptance criteria might be that the tested equipment must be able to remove all five 50-micron particles which are intentionally placed in a test bottle. It must be able to accomplish this for ten consecutive test runs conducted at 75°F and 80 percent relative humidity.

As an example of the usefulness of quality input to ensure that operating conditions are capable of preventing potential failure costs, take the case of a high viscous (flows with difficulty) liquid-like glue being filled into bottles. Because this type of product does not usually flow readily at ambient temperatures, it is not unusual to experience significant failure costs in the form of under- or over-filled bottles which must be salvaged. However, with quality assistance, a slightly elevated fill temperature might be found at which the product flows sufficiently to eliminate the undesirable variations in fill level and which is not detrimental to the product. Of course, this work would have to be done in conjunction with finding a suitable piece of bottle-filling equipment. This exemplifies the situation in which quality design input for operating conditions can contribute to profits by eliminating failure costs.

Sequence of Operations

A closely related factor is the *sequence of operations*. For example, for the packaging of bottled products described above, the capping operation should usually be performed as soon after the filling operation as practical in order to minimize the possibility of foreign material entering the product. Stated differently, very seldom would there be a valid reason for positioning another unit operation, like labeling, between the filling and capping operations. Another example for which the sequence of operations is important is the order of addition of ingredients for a product containing a fragrance. It is usually a good procedure to specify that the fragrance be added last, especially if the batch mixing is performed at an elevated temperature. This will minimize the amount of fragrance which is lost due to evaporation while the batch is being mixed.

Materials of Construction Requirements

Materials of construction (MOC) should be adequately tested for their expected application. Materials of construction are all the materials which are intended to directly contact a component or the product at some stage during the manufacturing process, but which do not actually become a part of the finished product. Stainless steel is the MOC when milk flows through a stainless steel pipe. To qualify for a particular use, a MOC must be tested from two perspectives under conditions simulating the manufacturing process: (a) the potential effect of the MOC on the component or product, which is the most important, and (b) the potential effect of the component or product on the MOC. Suppose that a soft drink is pumped from a storage tank through a plastic hose to a bottle-filling machine. Many plastics contain additives to give the plastic desirable properties. This soft drink, or any other liquid, has the potential to leach an additive(s) from the plastic hose. The result could be a disastrous effect upon the beverage's main attribute, its taste. Also, as the additives are deleted, the plastic can become brittle and crack or break. Therefore, the potential effects of the plastic on the soft drink and vice versa must be thoroughly checked out before the plastic is designated as an acceptable MOC for this use. Obviously, in this case and in most cases, the effect of the MOC on the component or product is the more important one, but both need to be considered. As an example of a situation in which the effect of the component or product on the MOC can be more important, consider the production in a steel tank of an aqueous solution of nickel sulfate for use in the electroplating industry. Although the nickel sulfate solution will corrode the steel tank, the small amount of steel which enters each batch of nickel sulfate should not substantially affect its use for electroplating purposes. However, with time, as the mix tank contacts many nickel sulfate batches, it is possible for corrosion to penetrate through the tank wall rendering it useless.

Auxiliary Material of Construction Requirements

Another factor closely related to the previous one is the desirable feature that an *auxiliary material of construction be safe and compatible with the product.* An auxiliary material of construction (AMOC) is a material which is not intended to directly contact a component or product during the manufacturing process, but which, under adverse conditions, could do so. An example is the lubricant used around the gears of a motor driving a top-entering mix tank agitator during the manufacture of a "sparkling clear" soft drink. The lubricant is not intended to contact the product in the vessel. However, if some of the lubricant does leak from the gear box, it could find a path down the agitator shaft into the soft drink. Even if just a few drops of this lubricant enter a batch of the soft drink, the batch may represent a failure cost in the form of scrap. This will be the result if there is any question whatsoever regarding the safeness of the batch for human consumption. Furthermore, many lubricants are dark in color, and this is hardly compatible with a soft drink marketed as "sparkling clear." These possibilities, which do happen, must be thoroughly assessed before the event actually occurs, so that the probability of this type of failure cost can be minimized. One of the most creative approaches that I have seen in this particular regard is the use of a product ingredient as the lubricant. For example, most lipsticks contain castor oil, mineral oil, and/or isopropyl myristate. Any of these are possible lubricants depending on the specific application. If one is suitable for a certain use, then even if a slight amount of lubricant does inadvertently enter the product, there is no concern relative to product safety or compatibility with the product.

A few years ago I experienced a rather unusual circumstance relating to an auxiliary material of construction. A consumer product was being manufactured in 32,000-pound batches. The finished product was a transparent yellow and highly viscous liquid. Material of construction tests had been conducted which demonstrated that, for the temperatures encountered in the process, this product was entirely compatible with 304 stainless steel. The processing system consisted simply of a 304 stainless steel mixing tank for blending the chemical components, three 304 stainless steel storage tanks for retaining the product prior to the packaging operation, a large 304 stainless steel pump which transferred each product batch from the mix tank to the appropriate storage tank, and the associated piping which also was made of 304 stainless steel. Each of the three tanks was capable of holding about 35,000 pounds of the product, each was equipped with a sampling valve for drawing off a product sample, and each possessed a vent which extended about 1 foot above the top of each tank. The purpose of the vent was to permit air to enter or exit the tank so that a pressure differential between the air on the exterior and the air inside the tank, which might cause the tank to collapse or rupture, could not be created. The vent contained a filter to prevent airborne foreign particles from contaminating the product. The only difference among the three tanks was that the mixing tank was equipped with an agitator in order to homogenize the components as the batch was being processed. Standard operating procedures specified that after any batch had been transferred to a storage tank, a sample should be obtained and sent to the laboratory. As soon as the laboratory determined that the batch adhered to its Finished Product Specification, it was released as acceptable for packaging.

Subsequent to start-up, the processing system had been successfully operated for more than 2 years without a major incident. Then, a sample taken from storage tank No. 1 revealed that the 32,000-pound batch which it represented was saturated with what appeared to be rust particles. Immediately thereafter, the top manheads were removed from the mix tank and storage tank No. 1. Using a flashlight, an inspection of the parts of the two tanks which were visible through the manhead openings indicated no apparent areas of rust and showed that the new, partially processed batch in the mix tank was void of rust particles. However, after the new batch was completed and transferred to storage tank No. 2, the sample sent to the laboratory revealed that this batch, too, contained an abundant supply of the rust particles. Immediately the making system was shut down. The two batches containing the rust particles were transferred from their storage tanks into 55-gallon drums. The mixing tank and storage tanks 1 and 2 were then thoroughly washed out and opened up. An inspector physically entered each tank. There was no evidence of rust on any interior tank surface. The remaining part of each lot of component which had been used in the two batches was inspected. No evidence of any significant quantity of rust or any other foreign material was detected in any of these component lots.

It was decided to attempt to process another batch of product. Plans were made to obtain a sample following each component addition to the batch. Each sample showed the batch to be free of the rust-particle enigma. When the 32,000-pound batch was completed, the sample of the finished batch obtained from the mix tank showed no rust particles. The batch was transferred to storage tank No. 1. The "official" batch sample was then obtained from this tank. It revealed that this batch was now loaded with rust particles! It was then reasoned that the problem source must be the transfer pump or the related piping. Once again the system was shut down. Disassembly of the transfer pump and an inspection of the piping disclosed no indication of any rust. A further inspection showed that the sampling valves were also rust-free.

At this point, an astute veteran staff manager announced that he could think of only one possible problem cause which had eluded investigation. He requested an operator to visually check the air vent on the mix tank. As soon as the operator viewed the interior of this vent, he knew the source of the problem. The 1-foot-long vent was made of carbon steel, not 304 stainless steel. The inside was filled with rust. Apparently, the tank designer or builder had concluded that since product would never directly contact the surfaces of the pipe, 304 stainless steel was not a requisite. However, over the 2-year period, the pipe had gradually corroded from normal exposure to the atmosphere until disaster struck. As the finished batch was being transferred from the mix tank to a storage tank, the air pressure inside the mix tank diminished as the liquid level decreased. Consequently, and as intended, fresh air rushed through the vent until the pressure inside the tank returned to atmospheric. At some point in time, the rust particles became sufficiently loose so that the air flow swept them into the product batch as it was being transferred to a storage tank. In retrospect, it was fortunate to have been able to pinpoint such a bizarre cause having produced only three unacceptable batches. The vent line was replaced with a 304 stainless steel section, and production was able to continue without further incident.

In net, 96,000 pounds of off-quality product valued at $0.26 per pound had been manufactured. Fortunately, it was determined that the rust particles could be removed from the contaminated product by filtration. However, due to the highly viscous nature of the product, the maximum filtration rate attainable with available equipment was 1500 pounds per hour. Thus, 64 hours were required to render all of this production free of the rust particles. An additional 15 hours were used in transferring the contaminated product from the storage tanks to drums. So, for approximately $1000 (79 hours × $12.50 per hour), $24,960 of product was salvaged. Other unquantified but significant failure costs were also absorbed as a result of the associated troubleshooting. In summary, all of the costs, lost production, and frustrations described above were the result of a 1-foot-long metal piece which never directly contacted the product.

Maintenance Needs

A decision must be made as to *whether equipment maintenance will be performed on a preventive or on an as-needed basis.* This decision can differ among various pieces of equipment. However, a "no decision" can be costly. Basically, this is an economic decision weighing the consequences of not performing maintenance until it is required versus the cost of providing preventive maintenance.

To illustrate, take the case of a fruit juice producer. Suppose that in transferring the juice from storage tanks to the can-filling machine a pump containing synthetic rubber gaskets is used, and that these gaskets upon prolonged contact with the juice harden and become brittle to the point of disintegrating. Assume that for a variety of reasons other gasket materials are not suitable. Suppose further, that the juice manufacturer knows from tests and experience that the useful life of these gaskets can range from 2 to 12 months in the fruit juice system. The juice manufacturer must then decide whether the cost of routinely replacing these gaskets every 2 months in order to prevent a quantity of juice from becoming contaminated with rubber particles is justifiable. The same decision may also apply to other equipment in this system which contains these gaskets. The decision should be made considering the probability of rapidly detecting contaminated product when gasket disintegration occurs, the cost of locating and segregating acceptable from contaminated product, the cost of scrapping or salvaging (e.g., by filtration, if the juice will not be affected) the quantity of product contaminated, the number of gaskets in the system and the gasket price, and the cost of maintenance personnel and lost production time to replace the gaskets. It is likely, in this case, that preventive maintenance is the better choice unless the gasket price is very high. Regardless, the point is that this factor must be considered and an intelligent plan agreed upon to prevent profits from being negatively affected.

Product Changeovers

When a manufacturing system is not used exclusively for a single product, it is important to *specify the procedure to be followed when changing from one product to another.* For example, if a lemon-scented, yellow rug shampoo and a rose-scented, brown floor wax are produced in the same equipment, residual traces of perfume and color from one product must be eliminated before starting to manufacture the other product. When an acceptable method has been determined for accomplishing a given changeover, it should be incorporated as a standard operating procedure.

Salvage Procedures

Procedures need to be established for salvaging subquality product. This will help ensure that the salvage operation is carried out economically and in such a manner as to prevent additional quality costs. For most occurrences of subquality product, the salvage procedure must be developed for the specific circumstance. Sometimes, however, a routine salvage procedure can be established. As an example of salvage via a routine procedure, consider the handling of recycled aluminum cans by an aluminum can producer. The concentration of recycled aluminum cans incorporated into new production batches has the potential of significantly altering the physical properties, such as tensile strength, of the new cans produced. Therefore, the aluminum can producer will probably specify that only x percent maximum of recycled cans is permitted in new production batches. This will prevent the production of unacceptable cans due to the presence of recycled material.

To illustrate a case when a temporary salvage procedure must be determined based on the specific circumstances, suppose that the manufacturer of a salad dressing produces two 50,000-pound batches which are unacceptable based on the company's standard for product flavor. Assume that the cause of these unacceptable batches has been identified and corrected. In order to avoid the failure costs associated with scrapping 100,000 pounds of product, the salad dressing producer will probably determine at what concentration the substandard product can be blended into new batches without affecting their flavor adversely. Then the procedure allowing the blending at, or up to, the specified concentration can be authorized. However, this authorization will expire as soon as the 100,000 pounds have been blended into new product. The procedure was authorized only for this particular off-flavor product because of a specific cause. If off-flavor salad dressing occurs again, it may be because of an entirely different cause and result in product which must be blended at a much lower concentration to avoid ruining the new batches. It is equally possible that this subquality product can be blended more economically at a higher concentration. Each situation must be handled individually.

Quality Standards

Another factor which needs to be considered is the *replacement of aging standards used to judge the acceptability of product or components*. This is particularly important for subjective tests like component or product odor, color, or appearance. For example, the producer of a men's after shave lotion will probably want to evaluate each production batch for fragrance acceptability. For this purpose, a sample judged to be acceptable by appropriate personnel will probably be used as the standard. Depending upon the intrinsic properties of the product and the environmental conditions in which the standard sample is stored, the fragrance of the standard itself may deteriorate with time. Provisions should be made to replace a standard of this type regularly and before it becomes unacceptable as a standard. If this is not done, it will become impossible to detect a component receipt or a production segment which is truly unacceptable for the attribute in question.

Review of Proposed Changes

It is very important to be certain that *any proposed manufacturing change be adequately assessed from a quality perspective before the change is implemented*. The purpose of this assessment is to ensure that adequate precautions are taken to prevent an unexpected escalation of quality failure costs when the operational change is instituted. We discussed in Chapter 3, "Components," the possible significant negative consequences on quality of a seemingly harmless process change without the benefit of a quality review. That discussion involved the installation of some copper piping in the manufacturing process by the supplier of a detergent for a rug cleaner. The same risk is present in the manufacturer's own operation.

One key item which should be included in the quality assessment of a proposed change is a determination of whether the proposed operation is consistent with quality reasons for conducting the operation in its current mode. To illustrate, suppose a producer of frozen vegetables warehouses the product in a large enclosed area where the thermostat is set to maintain −25°C. Suppose, also, that the frozen vegetables are shipped to customers in vehicles maintained at −20°C. The manager who is responsible for supervising the storage and shipping of this product reasons that if −20°C is acceptable during shipment, it must also be acceptable during storage. He or she determines that a very attractive annual monetary savings can be realized if the storage area thermostat is maintained at −20°C.

Now consider two possible scenarios. In the first, the manager and the boss agree that effective immediately the thermostat in the warehouse will be changed to a setting of −20°C. From their perspective, operations will not be affected in any way, and the cost savings is readily obtainable. In the second case, the boss is astute enough to ask the manager to ascertain why the thermostat was set at −25°C in the first place. Another properly directed question, or even better, a well-documented file reveals that the −25°C setting is required to prevent significant failure costs in the form of product spoilage and lost future sales. Because of air flow patterns, it is necessary to set the thermostat at −25°C to guarantee that all points in the large storage area are maintained below −18°C. So changing the thermostat setting to −20°C would not meet this criterion. In the smaller shipping vehicle, a setting of −20°C was determined to guarantee a temperature of less than −18°C. For the former case, very substantial failure costs would probably have been incurred. In the latter case, the proposed change would not have been implemented, and business would have proceeded normally.

Perhaps the best way to avoid an error of this kind is to have a formalized procedure which includes a quality assessment by qualified personnel for authorizing any proposed change in manufacturing operations. This includes laboratory and inspection operations.

The following example describes a rather unusual incident which I experienced some years ago. A product which we shall call a light brown, transparent pancake syrup was being manufactured by a continuous process at a rate of 20,000 pounds per hour. The system included several storage tanks for the major liquid ingredients, two pumps which transferred these liquids to the mix tank, a pump to transfer the product through a cooler and a filter to any one of four storage tanks, and appropriate instrumentation and controls. The cooler was a common shell and tube heat exchanger. The filter was a motorized, self-cleaning model consisting of many extremely thin metal sheets accurately positioned so as to remove particles 40 microns or larger. Sales for this product had greatly improved throughout the previous year. Anticipating further growth of the brand, management personnel from the process area in which the syrup operation was located determined that the production rate could be increased to 30,000 pounds per hour merely by installing a larger and faster pump to transfer product to storage. A pump of the required size and constructed of a suitable material was available in their inventory of spare parts. The pump was installed over a weekend shutdown.

On the following Monday, the slightly altered system started up without problems. During the first 5 hours of production the expected 150,000 pounds of pancake syrup were produced. Then a quality inspector reported that a number of bottles which had been found in the packaging operation contained a few very small but sharp pieces of metallic shrapnel. The entire operation was temporarily halted. Investigation revealed that the shrapnel was randomly distributed through all of the 30,000 pounds already filled into bottles and all of the remaining 120,000 pounds in storage tanks. Further investigation disclosed that the interiors of the self-cleaning filter had disintegrated, shattering into what appeared to be a great many very small, sharp metal pieces. Additional research divulged that the particular make and model of filter had a rated capacity of only 25,000 pounds per hour for a liquid of the density of this pancake syrup. Because of the small size of many of the metal pieces, there was much concern that even filtration would not guarantee that 100 percent of them would be eliminated from the product. This concern, coupled with the fact that this product would be orally ingested, lead to the decision that all 150,000 pounds would have to be scrapped. The bulk and packaged product were respectively valued at $0.12 and $0.25 per pound. The total failure cost from scrapping was $21,900. (Actually this is relatively inexpensive when one ponders the potentially astronomical failure costs which might have been incurred had the product been used by consumers.)

Would this failure cost have been averted if quality personnel had been consulted before action was initiated? The answer to this question will never really be known. However, had a formalized procedure for authorizing manufacturing equipment changes been used, at least an opportunity would have existed for experienced and judicious quality and engineering personnel to have reviewed the proposed change. Many relevant checklists which I have seen contain a question such as, "Will all associated equipment accommodate the proposed change?"

The following example is presented to demonstrate the more general need for a thorough quality evaluation of a proposed manufacturing facility, equipment, or procedure change. Suppose that a white wine producer's packaging operation functions at 100 bottles per minute because the bottle-filling equipment cannot operate faster. Operations management determines that an annual cost savings of $500,000 can be realized if the line speed is increased to 300 bottles per minute. Engineering determines that a filler which meets the requirements can be purchased for $100,000, and that the remaining equipment is already capable of operating at 300 bottles per minute.

At this point, it is necessary to evaluate the potential for increased quality failure costs for the new operating conditions. The types of questions which need to be considered include: Will the defect level increase at the elevated line speed? Will automatic quality equipment, such as a checkweigher for bottle fill weights, operate with the same effectiveness at the higher line speed? In other words, is there a difference between the two line speeds in the fraction of the units with an unacceptable fill weight which will be detected and rejected? At 300 bottles per minute, it will be quite difficult for line personnel to visually detect and remove unacceptable bottles. If this type of appraisal is an important aspect at 100 bottles per minute for preventing defects from reaching consumers, what alternate plans need to be incorporated to provide the same protection?

These questions can usually be adequately answered by judgment and trial runs under the proposed operating conditions. Based on the results, appropriate actions can be instituted to maintain failure costs at an acceptable level. However, failure to fully assess the quality cost ramifications of a proposed operational change can result in significantly increased quality failure costs which completely nullify anticipated monetary gains. Even worse, a higher net operating cost could result. A situation of this nature is illustrated in Chapter 9, Case C-10.

Personnel Training

The single most important factor which must be effectively accomplished in any manufacturing operation is *personnel training*. A great amount of money and effort is required to develop facilities, obtain equipment, and establish procedures to prevent failure costs. However, all of this money and effort is purely academic unless personnel are well schooled in the operation of the equipment and in the procedures to be followed. When operating personnel understand the procedures, quality goals can be met under normal conditions. However, when operating personnel understand both the procedures and their intent, quality goals can be achieved even under the abnormal situations which frequently occur in a manufacturing environment. The role of continued training and review to assist in preventing manufacturing errors cannot be overemphasized.

As an example of the benefit of operations personnel understanding the purpose of procedures, consider the producer of large batches of an expensive product which includes a granular thickener. Assume that during the batch-making procedure, several minutes are required in order for each particle of the thickener to wet out and then dissolve in the product. When this occurs, the product becomes a rich, thick cream. If the granular thickener is added slowly, the initial particles become wetted and dissolve normally. However, by the time the final quantities of the thickener are added, the product has become too thick for these particles to be adequately mixed in, wetted out, and dissolved. The net effect is a product which contains lumpy particles and which is not as thick as it should be. In order to prevent this occurrence, each batch maker who participates in the making of these batches is instructed to "add the thickener rapidly." Then all particles can become effectively mixed, wetted out, and dissolved simultaneously in a relatively thin solution. Now suppose that for any reason (e.g., humidity) some of the thickener being used has agglomerated into large lumps. The effect of adding this material rapidly would be almost identical to granular material added slowly. The external surfaces of the lumps would become wetted and dissolve, thereby initiating product thickening. The freshly exposed surfaces of the lumps would then have more difficulty wetting and dissolving. This would become increasingly difficult as more thickener dissolved. If, however, the batch maker understood why the granular thickener needed to be added rapidly, there is a reasonable chance that upon seeing the lumpy thickener, he would realize the potential problem and seek supervisory advice. The failure costs associated with this batch, or batches, could probably be avoided.

Degree of Documentation

Another factor which must be considered is the *degree of documentation of quality instructions*. These instructions include the product recipe, operating procedures, component and product sampling techniques and frequencies, laboratory test methods, quality inspection methods, salvage procedures, sanitation procedures, maintenance procedures, and so on. In almost all circumstances a sufficient amount of formal documentation is necessary for all procedures in order to minimize the probability of error due to miscommunications. Documents of this nature should be thoroughly reviewed by appropriate quality and operations personnel before being authorized. A formalized write-up of a procedure also provides a valuable training tool. Furthermore, it can serve as a standard against which actual operation can be compared to ensure that the procedures are actually being carried out in the intended manner.

Unique Circumstances

The final factor which must be considered for this area of responsibility is an examination of the overall manufacturing operation for *unique circumstances*. Because of the myriad of diverse products and manufacturing operations present in today's modern world, there is no way in which a general approach can be certain to include all pertinent factors to be considered. Therefore, personnel who have expertise regarding the specific product and manufacturing operation should search for potential events unique to their particular product-operations system which must be prevented.

Summary

There are a number of fundamental factors that need to be considered for a manufacturing operation in order to determine economical means of preventing quality failure costs. These factors are:

1. The accuracy and precision of the process
2. The degree of sanitation required
3. The design of each unit operation

4. The sequence of operations

5. The selection of materials of construction

6. The selection of auxiliary materials of construction

7. The usefulness of preventive maintenance

8. The procedure to be used for product changeovers

9. The procedures for salvaging subquality product

10. The replacement of quality standards before they deteriorate to an unacceptable point

11. The procedure for ensuring a thorough quality assessment of any proposed manufacturing change

12. Personnel training

13. The degree of documentation of quality instructions

Also, every manufacturing system should be examined for unique circumstances which could result in excessive quality failure costs if preventive action is not taken.

PREVENTION AND APPRAISAL MEASURES AS INSURANCE AGAINST UNEXPECTED FAILURE COSTS

In Chapter 2 through 4 and until now in this chapter, we have stressed the importance of actions aimed at preventing excessive quality failure costs. We reemphasize that *prevention is the best means for controlling product variability*. However, it is virtually impossible to anticipate all possible adverse eventualities that can occur. Furthermore, it is virtually impossible to guarantee that all preventive measures are always operating exactly as intended. Therefore, it is normally wise to utilize quality appraisals such that if a quality problem does occur, it will be detected quickly before failure costs can mount.

Also, there are a few circumstances for which quality failure costs can balloon completely out of control. An example is the failure cost associated with a product recall, which is discussed later in this chapter. For these circumstances, it is judicious to incorporate procedures which can restrain the potential total failure cost to at least a manageable level. These procedures are preventive measures in that their objective is to reduce failure costs. (Refer to the definition for preventive costs in Part I.) However, these preventive measures differ from all other ones discussed in that they are useful only when an actual quality problem occurs.

The purpose of this section is to discuss the *factors that should be explored to ascertain adequate appraisal and preventive measures to protect against unexpected, significant quality failure costs.* In other words, these measures constitute an "insurance policy" against incurring failure costs which could be harmful, or even catastrophic, to the firm's profit picture.

Appraisal Frequency and Location

The first factor to be examined is the *degree and location of quality assurance checks within the manufacturing operation.* The degree of quality assurance checks involves the frequency of sampling, the number of samples to be examined, and the selection of attributes to be checked. These items are basically determined by the unit manufactured cost of the product, the production rate, and statistics. Statistics for quality control and assurance is by itself the subject matter of many entire books. For this reason, we shall not even attempt to treat the subject within the confines of this book. Suffice it to say that statistics is an essential tool for helping to optimize the control of product variability. For an in-depth discussion of this topic, a multitude of valuable references are readily available.

Appraisals yield the greatest benefit when they are concentrated at points in the manufacturing operation at which failure costs could subsequently proliferate rapidly if failures are not prevented or quickly detected. There are three general points in a manufacturing operation where this situation often exists.

When Components Are Received

When a component receipt that does not conform to specifications is accepted and used, the resulting finished product may be unacceptable. Since manufacture of the product usually involves the combination of the defective component receipt with a number of acceptable receipts of other components, the cost of the finished goods can be manyfold greater than the cost of the defective component receipt by itself. Furthermore, the cost of unacceptable components is the responsibility of the supplier. However, the cost of unacceptable finished product using an unacceptable component is usually at least in part the manufacturer's responsibility.

Prior to an Operation Which Significantly Increases the Product's Value

Another point is immediately prior to any operation which substantially increases the monetary value of the product and the cost of salvaging unacceptable goods. An example is the packaging operation for a women's expensive perfume in an expensive package. Suppose that the perfume is manufactured in batches. If it is determined after the entire batch is filled into bottles that the perfume possessed an off odor, then the cost of the expensive packages has been added to the cost of the unacceptable product. If the odor of the batch had been assessed before packaging commenced, the malodor would have been discovered. In many cases, a batch of this kind can be salvaged simply and inexpensively by blending it at low concentrations into new batches of the product. However, once the product is filled into bottles, the cost of salvage includes the unpackaging and emptying of each individual bottle and probably the washing of the individual bottles to delete the off odor. Special operations like these can be very expensive.

Before Shipping Finished Product

Finished product appraisals should be sufficient to yield a very high confidence level that the product is acceptable. If a quality problem is detected subsequent to shipment, the producer must either absorb the customer-related failure costs (e.g., lost business or injury litigation) or incur the usually substantial costs and adverse publicity associated with a product recall.

In addition to these three general points for appraisals, particular circumstances can, of course, dictate appraisals at other strategic locations.

Sampling Plans

Numerous types of sampling plans have been created for conducting appraisals in manufacturing operations. The most commonly employed ones are probably single and multiple acceptance sampling by attributes and, to a lesser extent, acceptance sampling by variables. Also, ways have been developed for evaluating the quality data which appraisals generate. Perhaps the most widely used one involves the use of control charts. Just as for statistics, a myriad of useful books and other references already cover the subjects of sampling plans and quality data evaluation in sufficient breadth and depth that it would be redundant to include such a comprehensive discussion in this one. However, before proceeding to the next topic, I will digress momentarily to mention one aspect of the general application of appraisal programs which may not be universally practiced.

At the time a producer initially incorporates a component acceptance sampling plan into his manufacturing operation, the plan normally satisfies a real need and is economically justifiable. As time progresses, it is not unusual for a competent component supplier to substantially reduce his defect level. This can occur as the supplier learns how to manage his or her operation more effectively and learns what the customer really needs. However, it is not difficult for a producer to get caught up in the daily production pressures for acceptance or rejection decisions relating to individual receipts of the component and to neglect to monitor the overall defect level of the component. Thus, the producer may not be cognizant of a supplier's substantial defect level reduction. In the extreme, the supplier's production of components improves to the extent that 100 percent conforms to the manufacturer's acceptance criteria. For this circumstance, the manufacturer is perfectly willing to use every receipt of the component for production. Therefore, the component acceptance sampling plan is then providing virtually no benefit, but it is still costing the same amount as when it was originally introduced. All that is really needed at this point is a very small sampling of this vendor's material so as to detect any deterioration in quality performance. If this should occur, the more extensive original sampling plan or a more appropriate one can be reinstated. The point of this discussion is simply that in order *to avoid excessive expenditures for component appraisals, it is necessary to continuously monitor the overall quality being furnished by each component supplier*. It is probably already evident that this same discussion also *applies to a manufacturer's own finished product appraisal program*.

Let's examine the same point from a different perspective. Consider a discrete component (e.g., electronic transistors) being supplied to a manufacturer (e.g., of TVs). The transistor vendor and the TV manufacturer will ratify a component acceptance sampling plan. This plan serves as the basis for the TV producer's decision to accept or reject receipts of components. In classical statistical acceptance sampling-plan parlance, the vendor and the producer first agree upon an acceptable quality level (AQL). The manufacturer is willing to accept every component shipment which has a level (percentage) of defective units at or lower than the AQL. However, the sample acquired to evaluate any individual component receipt may not depict the true level of defective units in the shipment. For this reason, the vendor agrees to assume an α risk. The α risk is the probability that a component shipment which actually possesses a level of defective units equal to the AQL will be rejected by the producer, because the sample indicated a greater level of defective units. Second, the vendor and the producer will also agree upon a lot tolerance percent defective (LTPD). I shall refer to this as the unacceptable quality level (UQL). The manufacturer would prefer to reject every component shipment which has a level (percentage) of defective units at or greater than the UQL. However, the actual sample will not always reflect the true level of defective units in a receipt. Therefore, the manufacturer agrees to a β risk, which is the probability that a component receipt with a true level of defective units at UQL will be accepted by the manufacturer, because the sample exhibited a lower defective level. The remainder of this discussion deals with the β risk.

Assume that the TV manufacturer has agreed to a 2 percent β risk. The interpretation of this probability is that, for a component receipt which has a true defective level at UQL, the TV manufacturer incurs a 2 percent risk of accepting it. (That is, owing to chance alone 2 out of 100 such receipts will be accepted.) However, the β risk is pragmatically meaningless. The risk which the manufacturer needs to assess is not the risk of accepting a receipt at UQL (β risk), but rather the risk of *using* a receipt at UQL. This risk of using a receipt at UQL depends *both* on the risk of obtaining and the risk of accepting such a receipt. (Stated mathematically: $P_u = P_o \times P_{a/o}$; where P_u = probability of using a receipt at UQL; P_o = probability of obtaining a receipt at UQL; $P_{a/o} = \beta$ = probability of accepting a receipt at UQL given that one has been obtained.) If the vendor never manufactures a production segment having a defect level at or above UQL, the manufacturer will never obtain one. For this circumstance, therefore, there is no practical risk to the manufacturer of using a component receipt at or above UQL, *regardless of the value of the β risk*. (Mathematically: $P_o = 0\%$; $P_{a/o} = \beta = 2\%$; so $P_u = P_o \times P_{a \cdot o} = 0\% \times 2\% = 0\%$.) Yet, if the manufacturer is not aware that the risk (probability) of using a component at UQL is 0 percent, he or she will continue financing the acceptance sampling plan while obtaining no benefit from it.

In order to be able to assess the risk of using a component receipt at UQL, a manufacturer must know the β risk, which is determined via the acceptance sampling plan; and the probability of obtaining a shipment at UQL. The best method for a manufacturer to know the probability of obtaining a receipt with any given level of defective units is to monitor the overall quality level (mean and standard deviation) being supplied by the vendor. It should be noted that the vendor has an intrinsic motivation for manufacturing production segments below AQL, which, of course, is lower than UQL: By doing so the vendor reduces the risk of having a lot rejected which was in reality acceptable. Finally, this same discussion also has application to the manufacturer's finished product sampling program. The only difference is that the "risk of using" becomes the "risk of shipping product into the market." In other words, the β risk—the risk of shipping product with a defective level at UQL—becomes virtually meaningless when the manufacturer always manufactures product with a defective level below his or her own UQL for the product.

Automated Appraisal Equipment

The use of automated quality assurance equipment should be fully considered in order to fulfill a manufacturer's appraisal needs. Utilization of equipment of this nature involves a one-time, and in many cases relatively small, capital cost as opposed to the repetitive cost for an inspector to accomplish the same task.

To illustrate, consider cough medicine being filled into bottles and labeled on a packaging line operating at 150 bottles per minute. For obvious reasons, a bottle shipped into the market without a label is unacceptable, especially for a medicinal product like this one. However, a simple electronic eye device which can detect a bottle without a label and relay a signal to have it ejected from the operation can be designed and installed on a packing line for usually less than $15,000. Taking into account today's cost for labor, an inspector who watches for and physically removes the same bottles from the line might be remunerated at a rate of $20,000 annually.

Post-Manufacturing Appraisals

A closely allied and quite important factor to be evaluated is the *need for appraisals subsequent to completion of the manufacturing operation*. A number of circumstances exist that can cause failures that were not present, or at least not detectable, at the time manufacturing was completed to be present, detectable, and objectionable at a later time. To the greatest practical extent, these potential circumstances should be anticipated and confronted during the design of a product and its manufacturing system. Appropriate preventive measures should be enacted to eliminate, or at least minimize, their probability of occurrence. However, should any of these circumstances elude the quality system, they can lead to *in-transit*, *insidious*, and *in-use* failures. Each of these will be discussed in some detail below. In significant numbers, these types of failures can be highly detrimental to the profits of a business, especially when they wind up in the hands of the ultimate users. Therefore, as insurance against incurring substantial failure costs due to these types of failures, a marketer should consciously evaluate the need for appraisals beyond the manufacturing site. The desirability for, frequency of, and location of these types of appraisals must be determined based on a marketer's specific situation, but it is difficult to conceive of a situation in which at least some feedback would not be advantageous.

It is, in general, true that the cost for product appraisals increases as the time after and distance from completion of the manufacturing operation increases. To illustrate, consider that while the actual manufacturing process is in progress, it is relatively simple to appraise the product. Usually, a representative sample can be readily acquired and evaluated via a visit to the location of the operation. To obtain a representative sample from the same production segment after it has been warehoused will normally require specialized materials handling equipment and considerable time. Then the samples must be unpackaged in order to be evaluated. Once the product has been distributed to customer warehouses, the same considerations are present but in plural form. In addition, permission must be granted by the customer(s) just to obtain the sample. Finally, after the product is in the hands of the ultimate user, it can be very costly, time-consuming, and tedious to acquire product appraisal information. Despite these hardships, appraisals of these kinds should be considered for the reasons given above.

In-Transit Failures

In-transit failures include any failures which occur because of the shipment or handling of finished product at or beyond the manufacturer's warehouse. During product design, test shipments can be valuable in finding out how to adequately protect the product against normal storage, shipment, and handling conditions. During actual marketing, surveys of retail outlets for consumer products or remote warehouses for industrial products at regular intervals can uncover product mishandling. Once, I viewed a large shelf display of house paints in a retail store. One brand stood out like a sore thumb. Forty percent of the cans contained enormous dents covering one-third to one-half of the can surface and extending inward up to two inches toward the center of the can. These badly deformed cans at such a high incidence level would almost certainly have been detected at the manufacturing site if the damage had taken place at that location. The management of this company might not even be aware of these potential market failures. Immediately adjacent to the badly deformed cans were displays of several other brands, each showing only minor dents at a 3 percent to 5 percent incidence level.

Another illustration of in-transit failures is the spoilage of meat products or fresh produce owing to inadequate refrigeration during storage or shipment. A different kind of in-transit failure which some of us have encountered is represented by consumer (or industrial) products which are oil-in-water emulsions. A number of product categories including body lotions and several kinds of food products are of this nature. Basically, an oil-in-water emulsion is a suspension of droplets of an oily type of chemical in water. Because the oily substance is inherently insoluble in water, these products are naturally unstable. That is, the oil droplets have a natural tendency to coalesce so as to form a distinct separate layer which floats on top of the remaining water phase.

This tendency can be greatly accelerated by extreme environmental conditions, such as freezing temperatures. For a skillfully designed emulsion product, under typical environmental conditions this phase separation will occur so slowly so as not to be visible during the expected lifetime of the product. In many cases, it is relatively easy to protect a product of this type from the elements. For example, if it is known that temperatures below 32°F will freeze the product and cause it to separate into layers upon thawing, measures can be instituted to ensure that heating facilities are available during storage and shipment to prevent the product from attaining this low a temperature. On the other hand, protective measures are in many cases not economically justifiable against all possible eventualities which might "break" the emulsion. For example, consider an emulsion product which breaks at 120°F. It would be very difficult to justify the premium costs associated with requiring the shipment of all loads of this product in vehicles equipped with refrigeration facilities in order to avoid the one or two times each year when the vehicle interior might actually attain 120°F. Furthermore, emulsions are tricky products, and sometimes all the conditions which can cause the emulsion to break are not even known. However, when separation of the type described here does occur, it can be characterized by a line of demarcation which separates two unattractive, dissimilarly colored layers. For product on retail store shelves, this can influence a potential customer's choice of brands, particularly if the unattractive, separated product is positioned immediately adjacent to competition which has retained its homogeneity. Therefore, it is usually wise to consider market appraisals to monitor for in-transit failures. (For some products, like certain kinds of salad dressings, all of the competition undergoes a natural, rapid separation. For this situation, all the skillful designer can hope to do is to minimize the unattractiveness.)

I am familiar with one emulsion product which had been nationally distributed for several years without a major occurrence of phase separation. The product was packaged in a transparent bottle. Then a routine market appraisal one August revealed that a substantial amount of this product in Arizona retail outlets had not only separated, but the top, oily layer had solidified. That is, the melting point of the oily phase was above room temperature. Previous product testing had demonstrated that this phenomenon could in fact occur if the product was held at a temperature of 110°F or above for 3 days or more. Apparently this unlikely event had transpired. A decision was made to exchange acceptable units for solidified ones wherever these were discovered. It was reasoned that the failure costs associated with exchanging the units and scrapping the unacceptable ones would most probably be much less than the potential failure costs associated with a large number of users purchasing or just seeing this in-transit failure and becoming disenchanted with the product. Additionally, it was judged that, based on this single incident over a several-year period, invoking a procedure to store and ship all production in refrigerated vehicles was not warranted. To the best of my knowledge no further major incidents of phase separation have occurred.

Insidious Failures

Insidious failures only become present or detectable gradually as the product ages. To protect against this type of failure, it is often prudent to include some degree of delayed inspection and testing in the appraisal format. The potential value of this type of appraisal was demonstrated in Chapter 3 by the episode of the product which developed purple spots as it aged. Tests which significantly accelerate the aging of a product and for which the time correlation is known can be extremely useful for detecting insidious failures. For instance, if a producer of mayonnaise knows that aging it at 130°F for 96 hours yields the same product color and flavor change as experienced by the mayonnaise in 9 months under normal market conditions, the 96-hour test can serve as a valuable predictive tool for assessing typical production segments for abnormal changes. Periodic surveys of retail stores for consumer products and warehouses or storage tanks for industrial products can also furnish useful data.

Recently, while in a large automotive supply store, a display of motor oil caught my attention. Four of the leading brands occupied a large area of shelf space. All brands were stacked six units high with cardboard separating each layer. For three of the brands the display appeared normal. However, for the other highly advertised brand the cardboard appeared wet. Closer examination revealed that it was saturated with oil. Some of the cans possessed small oil droplets on their exteriors. About 15 percent of the units contained what appeared to be very small leaks at the can seam. It is probable that when this segment of production was inspected by the marketer, the leakage was invisible. Given three major brand alternatives with no price differential, would you purchase an oily or a dry can?

A large number of possibilities exist which can cause or contribute to the occurrence of insidious failures. The following discussion describes one of the more interesting ones that I have witnessed. The product was a white, opaque gel which contained a chemical compound consisting partly of a metal (e.g., zinc oxide). It was decided to package and market the product in an aluminum tube. The aluminum tube adequately protected the product from the environment, it permitted the product to be dispensed in the intended fashion, and it was readily available at a reasonable cost. However, it was known that if the product directly contacted aluminum, a chemical reaction would rapidly occur involving the metal compound in the product and the aluminum tube. The result would be a dark deposit on the surface of the white product. To prevent this, a design decision was made to have the interior of every aluminum tube thoroughly spray-coated with a polymeric material proven to be safe for the planned application. In addition, many preventive measures were incorporated, and automated and manual appraisals were widely employed at both the tube supplier's location and the product manufacturing site to assist in ensuring that the tubes did indeed possess an adequate coverage of the polymeric substance. These actions were initiated because despite the facts that the chemistry of the metal compound–aluminum reaction was well understood and that the resultant dark deposit presented no real risk to the personal safety of product users, there was considerable concern that consumers who encountered such a deposit while using the product might surmise it to be contaminated.

Production of the coated tubes commenced, and it proceeded with no major obstacles. Subsequently, processing and packaging of the product began, and it too progressed without a major incident. The product was to be tested in a limited market. An extensive appraisal of the product in its final shippable form was completed before the trial market was initiated. Everything appeared fine. It was standard operating procedure to conduct a market appraisal 3 to 6 months after initiation of a market. A market appraisal consists basically of inspecting the condition of the product as it appears in retail outlets plus purchasing a sufficient number of units to test product performance via simulated or actual consumer use. The results from this specific market appraisal elicited both surprise and utter frustration by revealing that approximately 6 percent of the units in the retail outlets contained at least one significantly sized deposit of the dark material.

In retrospect, what appears to have happened is that some of the aluminum tubes were manufactured with very small discontinuities, probably pinholes, in the coating. These were not detectable by either the electronic or visual means being employed to appraise the tubes. Over a time span of weeks, or perhaps even months, the product was able to penetrate these very small discontinuities so as to contact the aluminum surface. Subsequent appraisals and testing clearly demonstrated that a fraction of the tubes did contain pinholes in the coating and that product did indeed slowly penetrate into these small openings (and to some extent underneath the coating).

The moral to this story is that a market appraisal did in fact uncover an insidious failure before the majority of the production involved had found its way to the point of potential maximum failure costs—in the hands of the ultimate product user. It is certainly true that it would have been far superior, and much less costly, to have anticipated and prevented this failure in the first place. Actually, the possibility was recognized and what at the time appeared to be acceptable preventive measures were enacted. However, detection of the failure at this point in the distribution chain provided an opportunity for a decision to prevent failure costs from skyrocketing completely out of control due to expanding consumer dissatisfaction. For this particular case, a decision was made to terminate packaging this product in aluminum tubes. This decision was premised on the judgment that there was no reason to believe that subsequent production would not contain the same insidious failure at the same incidence level. The sale of finished product which was either in warehouses or in retail outlets was allowed to continue because the product remained able to perform its planned function, and because it presented no personal safety risk to product users. This situation exemplifies the importance of detecting insidious failures as early as possible. Fortunately, this product was subsequently successful when marketed in a different package.

Many industrial and consumer products are warehoused and shipped in cardboard boxes. These boxes can themselves generate insidious failures if they are not properly designed. To illustrate, it is obvious that the box must be sufficiently strong to protect the product against at least the conditions expected to be experienced during warehousing and shipping. The strength of these boxes depends to a large extent upon the geometry of the box and the construction of the cardboard members. Their strength can be significantly reduced through water absorption as from hot, humid summer air. Therefore, if the boxes are not designed to account for this factor, and particularly if the product is to be stacked relatively high during storage, insidious failure costs can occur in the form of collapsed product stacks.

In-Use Failures

In-use failures occur while the product is being used. How many of us have become highly irritated by the breakage of a tube containing a product such as glue while squeezing it? How many of us have been greatly frustrated by an aerosol product, such as a spray paint or a waterproofing agent, which quits dispensing product while it is evident that a substantial amount remains within the can?

In-use failures relate to the concept of *product reliability*. Product reliability is the probability that a specific unit of a specific product will function as intended for a specific time period under specific environmental conditions. For products like the glue and aerosolized goods mentioned above, it is clear that users expect a 100 percent probability that each unit will function as intended under typical conditions until the product is exhausted.

There is, however, another entire class of products for which substantial differences of opinion exist regarding the user's expectations of the product's useful time period or the average time between repairs. This product class includes televisions, automobiles, furniture, upholstery, all electrical appliances, and clothes. For products in this class, users expect a 100 percent probability that each unit will function as intended under typical conditions for the user's perception of how long the product should function. Whereas one consumer of a 4-year-old car may become highly annoyed with the manufacturer when a new fuel pump is required, another consumer might consider this to be the normal life for this part. Thus, for this class of products, the marketer must be more closely attuned to users so as to be able to distinguish the boundary between production which most users consider acceptable and production which a significant number of users perceive as constituting in-use failures. For both product classes, sound product design and real or simulated product usage testing of production segments should be the principal preventive and appraisal measures employed, respectively, to avoid in-use failure costs.

The following episode relates the occurrence of a rather unique and costly in-use failure. The product was a highly viscous, red, transparent gel packaged in a plastic squeeze bottle. A widely used polymeric substance was employed in the product formula in order to give this product the desired viscosity. Polymeric materials used for this purpose are, in general, comprised of complex mixtures of complex molecules of differing molecular weights and other nuances. It is precisely for this reason that producers and users of polymeric materials are unable to chemically characterize these substances in a Component Specification in such a way as to ensure that every shipment of material is chemically equivalent to all others. Instead, they must usually depend upon a combination of chemical and physical property specifications and checks to provide reasonable confidence that all shipments are, to the required degree, chemically equivalent. Also, it is for the same reason that manufacturers who use this type of product thickener normally obtain the desired viscosity for their product empirically by permitting operations to vary usage of the substance within a defined range. In other words, product consistency is achieved by trial and (it is hoped very little) error.

Some years ago users of this particular product began complaining that when they removed the cap from the bottle to use the product, dark red liquid of very low viscosity, like water, dribbled out. Some users objected to using product with this viscosity; others were highly distressed that the liquid had dripped on to their clothes or carpet. A preliminary investigation revealed that the problem was restricted to particular production segments.

It is worth digressing at this point to emphasize a vital learning. *When the marketer of a consumer or an industrial product initially becomes cognizant of significant quality failures via feedback from product users, it is probable that quality failure costs will be quite high*, sometimes enormous, even if the source of the failures is immediately remedied. Usually, a large chunk of additional production has already been completed and is in the "pipeline": the manufacturer's warehouse, in customer warehouses or retail outlets, and in the hands of product users. This is one of the most important reasons why a producer should seriously assess the value of real, if practical, or simulated product usage testing on a continuous basis.

For the specific polymeric thickener being discussed, it was known that oxygen could degrade it into smaller molecules so that it possessed considerably less thickening ability. Subsequent testing demonstrated that the probable cause of the problem was oxygen reacting with the polymeric thickener so as to deteriorate it to the extent that water could separate from the product. The red dye, which is water soluble, apparently migrated to the water layer. It is probable that every time product was dispensed from the bottle, fresh air entered as the remaining product receded into the bottle. Then, between uses, the new oxygen apparently reacted with the thickener to generate the thin, red liquid. It was known based on years of testing and experience that this phenomenon was not intrinsic to the product formula. Therefore, it was reasoned that the polymeric material must have changed. However, all of its chemical and physical properties had continually adhered to the relevant Component Specification.

A more in-depth perusal of pertinent data did reveal that one physical property of the thickener had trended downward starting at about the same time as the first production which displayed the problem. Since this was the only clue available, the supplier of the polymeric material was requested to only ship material manifesting the previous range of values for this property. Fortunately, this was feasible (with a "small" price increase), and since the problem subsided it must be concluded that this was indeed the cause. Subsequently, the Component Specification for the polymeric thickener was modified, with the vendor's concurrence, to reflect that all future shipments would maintain the historic level of the attribute in question. In addition, a simulated usage test for the final product relative to the product thinning phenomenon was developed. However, by the time all was said and done, this specific in-use failure tallied failure costs penetrating into the seven-digit classification. The potential in-use failures had progressed to the user before they were discovered. At that time, a considerable quantity of production containing the failure was already in homes across the entire country. Much more of the production was in stores; still more was in warehouses; a significant inventory of the polymeric material already manufactured had been accepted and was in warehouses; finally, considerable time and resources were required to sort out the problem and to rectify it. All the while, a substantial percentage of the users of the product were experiencing this in-use failure.

In-transit, insidious, and in-use failures are, by definition, not present, or at least not detectable, until after completion of the manufacturing operation. Therefore, unless a marketer is absolutely certain that all conceivable failures of this type have been prevented or otherwise deterred, it is a sound business practice to fully evaluate the merits of appraisals subsequent to completion of the manufacturing operation.

Equipment, Scale, Instrument, and Device Accuracy Appraisals

A frequency should be established for checks to validate the accuracy of equipment, scales, insruments, and other devices used to control or ensure key manufacturing conditions or to appraise components and product against their respective specifications. This is obviously an appraisal measure. However, the consequences of randomly discovering, or even worse of not discovering, that equipment of this kind has been operating beyond acceptable accuracy limits for an unknown time can be very expensive or even disastrous.

To illustrate, consider a breakfast cereal packaged in boxes with a marked net weight of 454.0 grams (1.00 pound) each. Assume that packaging operates at a line speed of 300 boxes per minute for two 460-minute shifts per day with an average efficiency of 90 percent. This yields an average daily production rate of 248,400 boxes. Also, assume the product fill weight of ten randomly selected boxes is checked every hour using a common scale. These data are used to appropriately adjust the fill weight so that the average box contains 455.0 grams. The extra gram is to provide a safety margin against underfilling. Now suppose that the scale receives a hard, accidental bump from a box set down beside it. Subsequently, the scale indicates 450.0 grams for an object which actually weighs 455.0 grams. Consequently, the fill weights will be increased so that the scale reads 455.0 grams, when in reality the weight is 460.0 grams. In other words, the average cereal box is being overfilled by 5.0 grams. If the cereal costs $0.60 per pound to produce, this means that every day $1641 of product is being given free to consumers. If no program exists to validate the accuracy of this key scale, the monetary loss will probably continue indefinitely. (What do you think the potential failure cost items would be had the scale inaccuracy occurred in the other direction, so that the average unit of cereal was actually 5.0 grams light?)

It is interesting to note that this entire scenario can be prevented by the implementation of a very simple procedure costing essentially nothing. If an object known to weigh exactly 455.0 grams is made available, the person performing the hourly weight checks can place the object on the scale immediately prior to each hourly check. If the scale reads anything other than from 454.9 to 455.1 grams, appropriate personnel can be contacted immediately to make the necessary adjustments before any additional data are obtained.

A scale or an instrument can go out of calibration from a variety of causes including poor equipment design, improper installation, cleanliness of the environment, temperature, humidity, misuse, or abuse. Therefore, it is very important that checks and calibrations be conducted at frequencies which are adequate to ensure the continuing accuracy and precision of equipment used to control operating conditions or to appraise material against specifications.

Traceability

A very important factor to evaluate is the *need for traceability*. Component traceability is the ability to determine the identification of the components which comprise any given segment of production. Product traceability is the ability to locate or identify any given segment of production at a later time. To illustrate, suppose that the Ace Motor Company was informed in March 1982 by its tire supplier that many of the tires made on October 25, 1981 and shipped to Ace November 13, 1981 possessed a defect which could result in a blowout. Hopefully, Ace's records were sufficient to show that these tires were used during a certain time frame, let's say from December 1 to 5, 1981. This is component traceability. For this particular circumstance, component traceability would only be beneficial if the Ace Motor Company's records were also able to identify the specific auto dealerships which received the cars assembled from December 1 to 5, 1981. This represents product traceability. It would have been additionally helpful if the records at these dealerships were able to identify the customers who purchased the cars. Even in this case, significant failure costs would be incurred, probably most by the tire company, to replace the defective tires. However, without component and product traceability, failure costs would have been greatly amplified in that the Ace Motor Company would probably have had to ask through the media that all purchasers of their 1982 cars bring them in to be inspected for the tire defect. Although traceability is not always required, it is important that every manufacturer understand the potential consequences of not having a traceability system for his or her particular product.

Records

Another factor which needs to be well thought-out in advance is the *type and amount of record keeping needed*. This is an area which can very easily and with significant extra costs proliferate beyond records that are really needed, to the point of being burdensome and costly, to finally just being bureaucratic in nature. In my opinion, record keeping should be initiated only for those items supported by a completely valid reason, and a review should occur at periodic intervals to determine if the reason remains valid. In other words, the records which are maintained should be minimized and controlled.

Basically, I can only think of five valid quality reasons which support maintaining a record:

1. To enable a review of the operation to ensure that it was as intended

2. To provide the capability for component or product traceability

3. To be available to assist in a troubleshooting analysis to detemine the cause of a quality problem

4. For legal protection

5. To comply with the law

In most cases, when reason **5** applies, one of the other reasons will, or at least should, also be applicable. As an example of an item for which it is very difficult to conceive of a situation in which records should not be maintained, consider any operation in which ingredients are homogenized into a batch. For reasons **1**, **2**, **3**, and **4**, and sometimes **5**, a record should be kept of the actual quantity and the lot number and supplier of each ingredient added to every batch.

Sample Retention

The usefullness of *retaining samples of finished product* should be considered for legal protection and for monitoring aged product characteristics. This can be especially beneficial in cases in which the product is manufactured in homogeneous lots. Imagine the case of a consumer who experienced, or claims to have experienced, badly swollen and blistered arms while using a product to relieve athlete's foot. Suppose the consumer's attorney notifies the manufacturer of the product that he or she intends to initiate litigation against the producer for inflicting bodily harm to the client. Sooner or later, the consumer will have to produce evidence showing that it was this manufacturer's product which caused the problem. Quite often the empty package will be presented. If the package contains a manufacturing code (traceability), and if a sample(s) of each code has been retained, chemical analyses and physical testing can be performed on the relevant sample to prove that the product which it represents was correctly formulated and that it did age in a typical manner (if this is, in fact, the case). It is probable that the manufacturer conducted some type of premarketing safety study demonstrating that the basic formula was safe for consumer use over its expected life. Therefore, with the retained sample data, the manufacturer's defensive position becomes much more formidable. Without the retained sample, the producer can only rely on records to demonstrate that the particular production was typical.

In many cases, it is judicious to monitor a product's aging characteristics under typical climatic conditions. The frequency of checks should be sufficient to rapidly detect a significant change in the expected aging pattern should one occur. Otherwise, if an undesirable change takes place, users might detect it first and cease using the product. For example, suppose a catsup producer discovers in mid-July that the flavor of the product made during the second week in June is deteriorating much faster than for normal production. Certainly, he or she will want to investigate the cause to prevent a recurrence. In addition, if the flavor is deemed sufficiently bad, the producer may choose to dispatch people to retail outlets to exchange acceptable product for the product in question. Of course, this can only be done if the catsup producer has the capability for product traceability.

Extra Appraisals During Start-Ups

During manufacturing start-ups, the utility of extra appraisals above and beyond what is expected to be necessary after the "bugs" have been ironed out should seriously be assessed. In the extreme case, start-ups involve a new product, a new manufacturing facility, new equipment, new procedures, new personnel, and new components. In every start-up something is new. It is impossible to anticipate all possible eventualities, let alone prevent them all. Also, it is highly doubtful that all preventive measures will operate exactly as intended from the very start. Therefore, it is smart to apply frequent appraisals at strategic locations to ensure that any quality problem is speedily uncovered so that failure costs cannot proliferate out of control. After obtaining a sufficient amount of operating experience to yield confidence that most potential quality problems have been prevented, these extra appraisal measures, and hence costs, can be decreased to a more tolerable level for continuing production. The extreme importance of product quality during a new or improved product start-up is dicusssed in much detail in Part III.

Personnel Training

Personnel training is a very important factor. This subject was covered in detail in Chapter 5.

Quality System Audits

A manufacturer relies heavily on the quality system to optimize the total quality cost by preventing excessive failure costs. It will become clear in Part III that failure to accomplish this can result in profits being deeply penetrated. Therefore, a manufacturer should evaluate the *merits of conducting periodic comprehensive audits of the quality system*. The purpose of a quality audit is to assess a part, or all, of a quality system's operation and adequacy. More specifically, a comprehensive quality system audit should determine if all unit operations and all quality recipe, operating, laboratory, and inspection procedures are being conducted and performed in the intended manner; and detect any deficiencies in the quality system. The comprehensive audit involves a thorough assessment of all phases of manufacturing including component receiving and storage, processing or assembly, packaging, product inspection, laboratory, warehousing, and shipping operations. The depth and frequency of a quality audit should be determined based on the probability of errors occurring; the potential consequences if errors do occur or if deficiencies exist; and the historical performance of the operation to be audited.

If it is decided that a comprehensive quality system audit is desirable, it is very important that it be conducted in a constructive manner. To maximize the probability of a competent and unbiased audit, an auditor (or a team of auditors) should possess technical expertise for the operation being audited, but should have no direct responsibility for the performance of the operation. An audit can be a highly beneficial tool when the auditor and operations management cooperate to approach the audit with the common goal of ensuring that the quality system's contribution to profits is optimized. The most effective audit procedure is for the auditor to conduct the evaluation by actually observing the operations in detail as they are performed. Deviations from intended operations and inadequacies in the quality system which are observed should be formally reported to operations management who have responsibility for implementing and reporting appropriate corrective actions. On the other hand, if the auditor approaches the job as a law enforcer, an audit can actually contribute to increased failure costs. In this situation, operations personnel can develop a contempt and disregard for those items which the auditor deems important.

A secondary purpose of a quality audit is to identify and eliminate antiquated operations and procedures. This removes unnecessary operating costs.

Summary

The factors a manufacturer should examine to determine appropriate actions as insurance against incurring unexpected, significant quality failure costs include:

1. The need for appraisals during the manufacturing operation

2. The need for product appraisals after the completion of manufacturing

3. Accuracy and precision validation checks for scales, instruments, and equipment

4. The need for component and product traceability

5. The type and quantity of records needed

6. The usefulness of retained component and/or product samples

7. Extra appraisals during start-ups

8. Personnel training

9. The usefulness of a manufacturing quality system audit

PART THREE
The Bottom Line

The ultimate goal of a quality system should be to optimize the total quality cost. Optimization implies preventing failure costs to the fullest practical extent and minimizing quality failure costs which do occur. When optimization is achieved, profits can be significantly enhanced. It is the objective of Part III to demonstrate the very substantial profits which can be obtained from a competently developed and efficiently managed quality system as contrasted with the potential annihilation of profits which can result from a nonexistent, incompetently developed, and/or a mismanaged quality system. This is accomplished in Chapters 6 through 10 by the presentation and discussion of four case studies which include: (a) the demise of a new product due to a virtually nonexistent quality system; (b) a very large loss of profit due to an insufficient quality system; (c) a smaller profit loss due to an excessive quality system; and (d) the realization of the quality function's optimum contribution to profits through the competent development and management of an efficient quality system. Although the actual case studies presented are hypothetical, they are premised upon real data and real events.

The other goal of Part III is to identify the traits which characterize profitable quality systems. This is accomplished in Chapter 11 by analyzing the lessons contained in the case studies. Identification of these traits can provide valuable clues for the successful development and management of profitable quality systems.

Prelude to the Case Studies

DEFINITIONS

Defects

Prior to embarking into Part III, several terms need to be defined as they will be used in the material to be presented. A "*defect*" is a product imperfection. Because different types of defects elicit different reactions from product users, it is important that the product defects be classified according to their potential for negative consequences. In this book, we shall define a *crucial defect* (*cd*) as one which renders a product unfit for use. Examples would include a garden hose with a hole, salad dressing containing a dead spider, a deck of fifty-one playing cards, a nonadjustable wrist watch that loses 10 minutes per day, an easy chair with a broken leg, and a light bulb which does not light. We shall define a *serious defect* (*sd*) as one which does not render the product unfit for use, but which does significantly detract from the product or tarnish the image of the marketer in the eyes of the consumer. Examples include a sofa with an upholstery flaw, a briefcase with a latch that is difficult to fasten, a box of cereal without the advertised prize enclosed, a power lawn mower that stalls frequently, and an expensive bottle of wine with an upside-down, frayed label. For the sake of simplicity, we shall restrict the case studies and their discussions to these two types of defects. However, actual practice will many times dictate the need for other defect classifications such as regulatory defects, which might include all violations of federal, state, and local statutes.

Internal Failure Costs

For the remainder of this book, it is necessary to separate quality failure costs into those that occur internally and those that occur in the market.

Internal failure costs can result from (a) disposing of subquality material while it is still at the manufacturing site and (b) being unable for a quality reason to manufacture acceptable production. For example, (b) would include the costs associated with manufacturing downtime due to the production of excessive defects; (a) would include the costs to blend subquality batches of bulk chemicals at low levels into new batches. Consider a lipstick manufacturer who completed a batch which was too dark to adhere to its finished product specification for color. The manufacturer determined via small laboratory batches that the subquality batch was able to be blended at 10 percent level into new batches of the lipstick so that the resulting product did meet the required color specification. The cost for preparing the small-scale batches was $25.00 in labor and $5 in material. The extra labor cost for the actual blending operation was $20 per batch. Therefore, the internal failure cost to salvage the off-color batch of lipstick was $25 + $5 + $200 = $230.

Another example of an internal failure cost is the expense associated with scrapping damaged goods. Suppose a lamp producer discovers that a forklift driver bumped into a stack of twenty-four lamps in the warehouse. Inspection of the lamps disclosed that it was not economical to salvage them. Each lamp had a manufactured value of $50. Also, it cost $100 in labor to clean up the mess in the warehouse. Therefore, the cost of this internal failure was $1300.

Still another type of internal failure cost is the expenditure for culling defectives from a segment of production. Assume that a marketer of AM-FM transistor radios determined that a lot consisting of 6000 radios contained 3 percent with a defective on/off switch. The inspector evaluated 300 radios in 1 hour, removing the defective units, and was remunerated at $10 per hour. To repair each of the defective 180 radios which were culled cost $3 in labor and $0.25 for the part. Thus, the internal failure cost for this salvage operation was:

$$\left[\frac{(6000) \text{ total radios}}{(300) \text{ radios inspected/hr}} \times (\$10) \text{ cost/hr} \right] +$$

[(180) number of defective units × ($3.25) cost/defective unit] = $785

Market Failure Costs

Market failure costs can result (a) from shipping subquality product into the market and (b) due to a quality reason, having no finished production acceptable for shipment to the market. An example of (b) is a bicycle marketer who cannot fill an urgent customer order for 100 ten-speed bicycles because his entire warehouse inventory of these bicycles requires a salvage operation to correct a safety defect. This gives the customer the "opportunity" to meet his urgent need by purchasing the 100 bicycles from a competitor. Examples of (a) include the costs associated with following up on complaints to the producer of defective flashlight batteries, costs to honor guarantees to repair defective dish washers during the first 3 months of use, freight costs related to the return of rejected shipments of bulk chemicals, product litigation costs, and the cost of lost profit due to customers becoming disenchanted with the marketer after purchasing defective product. This cost of lost profit because of user dissatisfaction with a product can devastate profits if it gets out of control. This point is clearly demonstrated in the case studies presented later in Part III. In the worst case, management is not even cognizant of the real reason that profit objectives are being sadly missed, since this cost does not normally appear in any accounting report. Therefore, it is imperative that the quality system somehow monitors this important cost and initiates and recommends actions as appropriate.

In order to effectively track this important cost, it is necessary to have information concerning the frequency of user reactions following the purchase of each type of defect. The product user has a number of options available: (a) request nondefective product from the manufacturer or retailer, (b) request repair via the product warrantee, (c) not purchase additional products made by the manufacturer, (d) complain to the manufacturer and/or retailer of the product, (e) take some other action, (f) take more than one action, or (g) do nothing. A variety of channels exist for a marketer to obtain insight as to the frequency of each of these reactions for a given product and a given defect type.

For producers of industrial products, this information is usually more readily accesible than for the producers of consumer goods. Whereas a single consumer brand might be used by millions of unidentified people, the users of a single industrial product are normally identifiable and consist of a much smaller number than with consumer products. Therefore, industrial product marketers have the capability of communicating with at least a significant number of their customers on a regular basis to discuss product quality (and any other pertinent topic).

For manufacturers of consumer products, perhaps the most accurate method of gaining knowledge of this kind is through market research involving house-to-house surveys. However, this approach can be quite expensive since most houses contacted will not even have experienced defective product or may not even use the product. An almost as effective but substantially less expensive approach involves the use of simulated defects in concert with panelists who are requested (or compensated) to use the product and to report on their likes, dislikes, and impressions. Another reasonably effective method for obtaining the needed information is via mail or telephone follow-up with consumers who have registered specific product complaints. This tactic serves the additional purpose of potentially providing some pacification to these irate or frustrated customers. In recent years, a number of corporations have introduced toll-free, call-in telephone numbers to meet all of these needs. Obtaining defect-reaction frequency information from consumers who have voiced specific complaints can result in data which are biased in a direction tending to show that the quality system is contributing less to profits than its real contribution. This bias could result in the introduction of a few additional quality measures which in reality are not needed. However, it is demonstrated in the case studies that until a quality system can be optimized, errors of overindulgence are much less expensive than errors of omission.

Finally, lacking real reaction frequency data of any kind, an educated guess by experienced and astute personnel will usually provide reasonable estimates for the reaction frequency for a particular product and defect type. This is also demonstrated in the case studies.

The Average Market Failure Cost

For any particular product, the best available information pertaining to the frequency of user reactions after buying defective product can be used in conjunction with the cost per occurrence of these user reactions to yield an estimate of the market failure costs for that product. This can be accomplished in a number of different ways. It is my opinion that the one which is the simplest to apply is the *average market failure cost for each defect type*, and for this reason this will be the technique employed for the remainder of the book. We'll denote the average market failure cost by $\overline{MF}_{yd}$ where the $\overline{}$ designates that it is an average value, and the y designates the defect type. For crucial and serious defects, the notations will be $\overline{MF}_{cd}$ and $\overline{MF}_{sd}$, respectively.

To assist in understanding the average market failure concept, consider the case of a manufacturer of stereos which retail for $200. Assume that this producer has acquired defect-reaction frequency data by one of the methods discussed above. The data show that for crucial defects, such as the unit manifesting chronic static in the left channel, the unit not receiving stations over 5 miles distant, or the unit not turning on, consumer reaction frequency and related costs are as follows:

> 100 percent return the unit for repair under warrantee or for exchange of the unit. The average cost to repair returned units is $25.

> 10 percent, in addition, will not purchase any more products

marketed by the company. The company estimates a $150 profit loss for each of these consumers.

20 percent, in addition, write a letter of complaint to the manufacturer. The average cost to follow up on each complaint is $1.50.

Therefore, using a basis of 100 crucial defects, the average failure cost for each crucial defect shipped into the market, $\overline{MF}_{cd}$, is computed by:

$$\overline{MF}_{cd} = \frac{(100 \times \$25) + (10 \times \$150) + (20 \times \$1.50)}{100 \text{ crucially defective units}}$$

$$\overline{MF}_{cd} = \$40.30 \text{ per crucially defective unit}$$

The interpretation of this value is simply that, on the average, every stereo unit which contains a crucial defect and which winds up in the hands of a consumer will cost the manufacturer $40.30.

Suppose the producer's data show that for serious defects, such as a dent on the front panel, the lack of operating instructions included in the box, or a wrong-colored knob, consumer reaction frequency and related costs are:

98 percent return the unit for repair under warrantee or for exchange of the unit. The average cost for repair is $4.

2 percent take no action.

5 percent, in addition, write a letter of complaint to the manufacturer. As with cd's the average cost to follow up on each complaint is $1.50.

Thus, the average failure cost for each serious defect shipped into the trade is calculated as:

$$\overline{MF}_{sd} = \frac{(98 \times \$4) + (2 \times \$0) + (5 \times \$1.50)}{100 \text{ seriously defective units}}$$

$$\overline{MF}_{sd} = \$4 \text{ per seriously defective unit}$$

It is usually desirable for a manufacturer to review the defect reaction frequency information at regular intervals as a check to ensure that it has not changed significantly. This is especially true in a rapidly changing environment, such as escalating inflation. As an illustration, consider the probable consumer reaction to a crucial defect for two entirely different products. A consumer who discovers such a defect in an expensive new automobile will, in virtually every case, request the deficiency be corrected at the manufacturer's expense. On the other hand, a consumer who obtains a crucial defect with a relatively inexpensive roll of breath fresheners (completely crumbled) may choose to ignore the situation after venting his or her anger. However, at some point, as the price of breath fresheners increases, the same consumer may become sufficiently disgusted with the wasteful purchase to switch brands. When this occurs, quality failure costs can increase very rapidly. *The price of a product can influence consumer reaction to quality failures.*

Preventive Costs

Following is a brief description of the manner in which expenditures for preventive measures will be treated in the case studies. As is the general rule, preventive costs will be allocated to the time period during which they are incurred. However, it must be recognized that this procedure will somewhat mask the true value of some preventive measures. This is because there are two kinds of preventive costs, continuing and temporary.

Continuing Preventive Costs

Continuing preventive costs (P_C) must be incurred repetitively during every time interval in order for the benefit of that expenditure to be realized in the respective time interval. To illustrate, suppose that a pharmaceutical company sterilizes one of its drug manufacturing systems every week in order to prevent failure costs associated with microbial contamination of the product. For the company to continue to receive the benefit of preventing a microbial problem, it must continue to spend money to sterilize the system every week.

Temporary Preventive Costs

Temporary preventive costs (P_T) are only incurred one time, but their benefits can be accrued for the entire life of the product. As an example, consider the cost to develop the Component Specifications for a product. This cost includes the salaries and related overhead of the personnel performing the work, travel expenses, materials needed, testing conducted, and so on. All of these costs cease when the Component Specifications are completed. The personnel can be transferred to other projects. However, these Component Specifications can assist in preventing the purchase and use of unacceptable components for many years to come. In the case studies, for simplicity, temporary preventive costs incurred during the development of the product will be assigned to the first year of production. Other expenditures of this nature will be assigned to the year during which they occur. This treatment of temporary preventive costs sometimes makes the expenditure appear high for the first year relative to the benefits derived. However, in subsequent years, the same benefits will be obtained from a zero expenditure.

THE PRODUCT AND THE COMPANY

This section will set the stage for the case studies by describing the company, the product, and the portion of the situation common to all four cases. Assume that the JEBB Beverage Company is a medium-size business located in the Midwest. JEBB currently markets two established soft drinks with a combined market share of 3 percent of the huge soft drink market. The company has initiated a development effort for a new soft drink which is to be a sparkling clear, peppermint-flavored, carbonated beverage. It is to be packaged in a clear, transparent glass bottle possessing a silkscreen label with a threaded aluminum closure. These units are to be packaged in convenient carrying cases of eight units each, which in turn will be packaged into shipping containers.

Marketing

JEBB's marketing department predicts sales of approximately 47 million gallons of the new product annually for the first several years of its existence. This is equivalent to about a 0.6 percent share of the carbonated beverage market. To simplify the case studies, we shall assume that all of this product will be produced and sold in 12-fluid-ounce bottles. This turns out to be approximately 500 million 12-fluid-ounce bottles each year. Assume that for the new product the average user will buy one eight-pack every 2 weeks. This equates to 208 bottles per year. Combining this information with the expected annual unit sales indicates that JEBB will have 2.4 million users of the new product.

JEBB intends to price this product at $0.43 per bottle. Manufacturing costs are expected to be $0.20 per bottle. This includes $0.10 for the product and $0.10 for the overall package. Of the $0.23 per unit selling margin, $0.10 is profit and the remaining $0.13 is to cover the costs associated with relevant marketing, sales, purchasing, legal, and other activities.

Manufacturing

Manufacturing intends to provide the required production by operating 4 packing lines, each at 500 units per minute with an expected efficiency of 80 percent. The lines will operate 250 days per year, 3 shifts per day, and 430 operational minutes per shift. This packaging operation will be supported by a product-making system consisting of a mix tank which can produce a 150,000-pound batch every 2 hours. The batch is prepared by mixing potable water, flavor and flavor enhancers, sweetener, and a preservative. The mix is then carbonated with appropriate temperature control and pumped to a storage tank. Eight 150,000-pound storage tanks with appropriate temperature control capability will be utilized. Each packing line will receive product exclusively from two of these storage tanks, so that while a line is packing product from one tank, the making system can fill the alternate tank.

Average Market Failure Costs

In order to obtain an estimate of the average market failure cost for each defect classification, assume that JEBB will utilize results from previously conducted market research studies of consumer reactions to specific defects for its existing soft drink brands. The results show that 67 percent of consumers who purchase a unit with a crucial defect will repurchase the brand, but the remaining 33 percent will elect not to repurchase it for at least 1 year. Also, 10 percent will write a complaint letter to the producer, and 0.002 percent will file legal charges against the company. For a serious defect, the average consumer will repurchase the brand 98 percent of the time and elect not to repurchase the brand for at least 1 year 2 percent of the time. Also, 1 percent will write a complaint letter to the producer. All of these market research results represent average figures per occurrence, independent of the number of times a consumer had previously bought a unit with a defect.

The expected profit which is lost when a customer discontinues purchasing the brand for one year is simply:

$$[(208) \text{ (bottles/yr)/lost consumer}] \times (1) \text{ yr} \times$$

$$[(\$0.10) \text{ profit lost/bottle}] = \$20.80 \text{ profit lost/lost consumer}$$

Upon receiving a written user complaint, JEBB sends the consumer a coupon valued at $3.44 for a free eight-pack. To follow up on each letter requires 6 minutes of clerical time and 3 minutes of management time. We'll assume that the cost including benefits and overhead is $25,000 per year ($12.02 per hour) for a clerk and $50,000 per year ($24.04 per hour) for a manager. Therefore, the cost of handling each complaint is given by:

$$[(\$3.44) \text{ cost/coupon}] + [(\$12.02) \text{ cost/hr} \times (0.1) \text{ hr}]$$

$$+ [(\$24.04) \text{ cost/hr} \times (0.05) \text{ hr}] = (\$5.84) \text{ cost/complaint}$$

Assume that previous experience has shown that the average total cost for legal action including fees and settlement cost is $10,000 per occurrence.

The average market failure cost for each defect classification can be determined by combining the above costs for particular consumer reactions to defective product with the market research data:

$$\overline{MF}_{cd} = \left[\frac{(33) \text{ lost consumers}}{(100) \text{ cd}} \times (\$20.80) \text{ cost/lost consumer}\right] +$$

$$\left[\frac{(10) \text{ complaints}}{(100 \text{ cd})} \times (\$5.84) \text{ cost/complaint}\right] +$$

$$\left[\frac{(0.002) \text{ lawsuits}}{(100) \text{ cd}} \times (\$10,000) \text{ cost/lawsuit}\right] = \$7.65 \text{ cost/cd}$$

Similarly,

$$\overline{MF}_{sd} = \left[\frac{(2) \text{ lost consumers}}{(100) \text{ sd}} \times (\$20.80) \text{ cost/lost customer}\right] +$$

$$\left[\frac{(1) \text{ complaint}}{(100) \text{ sd}} \times (\$5.84) \text{ cost/complaint}\right] = \$0.47 \text{ cost/sd}$$

Salaries, Wages, and Taxes

Assume that the cost to JEBB for one quality engineer is $50,000 annually and for an hourly plant employee is $25,000 per year ($12.02 hourly). Included are the costs to the company for administration of the quality system, for overhead, and for benefits. Also, to simplify the case studies, profits will be considered strictly on a "before taxes" basis. Inclusion of tax ramifications would unnecessarily complicate the subject matter. Finally, we shall assume that JEBB has tested their new soft drink among a sufficient number of potential consumers to be confident that the product possesses an acceptable degree of excellence. Consequently, from a quality viewpoint, all that remains is the control of product variability. For this reason the word "quality" and the phrase "control of product variability" will be used interchangeably in the case studies.

JEBB Data Summary

The stage is now set for presentation of the four cases. To facilitate reference while reading these case studies, Table 6-1 summarizes the key data and information for the JEBB Company's planned new soft drink.

TABLE 6-1.   JEBB Data Summary

Sales expected:	500 million bottles per year (12-fluid-ounce bottles)
Users expected:	2.4 million people (each buys 208 bottles per year)
Price:	$0.43 per bottle
Manufactured cost:	$0.20 per bottle ($0.10 product; $0.10 package)
Profit:	$0.10 per bottle
Production:	2 million bottles per day (total from four packing lines)
Average market failure costs:	crucial defects: $\overline{MF}_{cd}$ = $7.65 per cd
	serious defects: $\overline{MF}_{sd}$ = $0.47 per sd
Cost for a quality engineer:	$50,000 per year
Cost of a plant hourly employee:	$25,000 per year

7 Case A: The Death of a Brand

In this case, the JEBB Company did not regard the control of product variability as having prime importance. This attitude can stem from the belief that the product is so simple to manufacture that a negligible quantity of failures will be produced, or it can be due to ignorance of the magnitude of failure costs which can result when product variability is inadequately controlled. Regardless of the reason, product quality and, hence, product profits are placed in extreme jeopardy.

YEAR ONE (A-1) IN RETROSPECT

Prevention Costs

Preventive measures which JEBB considered necessary included $30,000 in temporary preventive costs for assisting in the design of manufacturing operations; the development of Component Specifications and related inspection techniques at a temporary preventive cost of $30,000; and the development of specifications and tests for finished product at a temporary preventive cost of $10,000. The only other preventive measure which JEBB deemed appropriate was to place a code on every case of product indicating the day on which the product was packed. When a quality problem occurred, production from the day involved was located, and appropriate actions were taken. The continuing preventive cost to obtain and change the codes each day was $2000 per year. Thus the total preventive cost, P, was $72,000. This consisted of $70,000 in P_T and $2000 in P_C.

Appraisal Costs

To appraise components and product, JEBB employed two full-time inspectors, each of whom could perform all the necessary chemical testing, physical testing, and inspection of units. Each of the four packing lines set aside six randomly selected cases of finished product per day. During the subsequent working day, one of the inspectors collected and examined the product contained in the twenty-four cases. Because of the company attitude towards the control of product variability, no inspections to cull defective units were undertaken. Actions were initiated only when a bulk product problem was discovered, since 100 percent of the represented production was involved. The inspectors also examined samples of component receipts. About 20 percent of the time, their inspection was completed prior to the component being used for production. The total appraisal cost, A, was $60,000. This included $25,000 for each inspector plus $10,000 in destructive testing costs. The latter refers to any costs incurred due to test procedures which destroy components or product to the extent that they cannot be used or sold, respectively, in the intended manner.

Internal Failure Costs

Prior to start-up, JEBB did not conduct a trial run to determine the potential of their manufacturing system for generating failures. The specific failures which were discovered at the plant during year one and the associated internal failure costs are discussed below:

1. Four times during the year, residual chlorine remained in the making and filling systems due to an inadequate water rinse following the required weekly sterilization. The mixing of the residual chlorine with the product had taken place randomly and frequently throughout the day. Product flavor was adversely affected. Even after the residual chlorine was later in the day entirely flushed from the system, the subsequent production had to be scrapped. This was because the problem was not discovered until the routine product examination on the following day. At that time, acceptable product could not be distinguished from unacceptable product: the code on each container of product identified the product only by day, not by time during the day. The cost of the four events was:

   (2,000,000) bottles/day × ($0.20) value/bottle × (4) days = $1,600,000

2. Five days during the year, the water purity was sufficiently poor to impart an off flavor and/or some degree of turbidity to the product. On 4 of those 5 days, the entire day's production had to be scrapped because virtually all units were of unacceptable flavor and/or clarity. Just as with the residual chlorine events, the problem was not discovered until the next day, and the cost of the four events was $1.6 mil-

lion. The fifth occurrence was deteched via component inspection prior to use. The entire operation was shut down for one day at a cost of only $3000.

3. On two days during the year, the scale used to weigh the flavor for each batch of the beverage gave erroneously high readings causing weakly flavored product to be produced. Again, the entire two day's production had to be scrapped. The product inspector did not ascertain until the next day, after the product had been filled into bottles, that the product was very weak in flavor content. The cost was:

$$(\$400,000) \text{ value/day} \times (2) \text{ days} = \$800,000$$

4. Five times during the year, empty bottles as received from the bottle supplier contained grease. For four of the five incidents the bottles were used in production. The resulting product was discolored and potentially unsafe. Once again the problem went undetected on all four occasions until the next day, and the entire day's production had to be scrapped. However, the bottle supplier did agree to absorb 50 percent of the cost since his plant was the source of the difficulty. Therefore, the cost to JEBB was:

$$\tfrac{1}{2} \, [\$400,000 \text{ value/day} \times (4) \text{ days}] = \$800,000$$

The fifth occurrence was uncovered by the component inspection plan prior to using the bottles. These bottles were rejected and returned to the supplier at no cost to JEBB.

5. $500,000 due to miscellaneous events.

The total cost of internal failures (IF) for the year was $5,303,000.

Market Failure Costs

The defects which occurred and which were shipped to the trade, thereby becoming market failures, were as discussed below:

1. As the filler introduced product into bottles, several defects were generated: (a) 0.15 percent of the units contained some lubricant which had leaked from the filler; although the lubricant was not toxic even if orally ingested, it presented the intended sparkling clear drink with a turbid, unappetizing appearance; (b) 0.40 percent of the bottles were filled to too low a level in the bottle; and (c) 0.60 percent of the bottles were sticky due to product which dripped from the filler on to the bottle exteriors. Of these defects, (a) was a crucial defect, whereas (b) and (c) were serious defects.

2. As the capper placed a threaded aluminum closure on each bottle, the following defects were generated: (a) 0.15 percent of the caps were applied too loosely resulting in product with weak flavor and no carbonation due to evaporation; (b) 0.80 percent of the bottles had closures which were very difficult to remove because they were applied too tightly; and (c) 0.25 percent of the bottles had necks which had been cracked due to closures being applied very tightly; the cracks were not visible since they were covered by the cap itself. Of these defects (a) and (c) were crucial defects, and (b) was a serious defect.

3. Large pieces of foreign material somehow entered the product in 0.10 percent of the bottles, while smaller pieces of foreign material somehow entered the product in 0.50 percent of the bottles. The former were classified as crucial defects, while the latter were serious defects.

4. A variety of serious defects due to label flaws occurred at 0.30 percent.

5. Miscellaneous crucial and serious defects occurred at incidence levels of 0.10 percent and 0.40 percent respectively.

Considering all of these defects, 0.74 percent of the bottles were produced with a crucial defect and 2.95 percent with a serious defect. A summary of these defects is shown in Table 7-1. Since all of these defects were shipped into the market, they all became "average" market failures. The logic behind shipping all of this production as opposed to some other alternative is discussed in detail shortly.

The cost of market failures due to crucial defects was:

$$(.0074) \text{ cd/bottle} \times (500,000,000) \text{ bottles/year} \times (\$7.65) \text{ cost/cd}$$
$$= \$28,305,000$$

It is important to note that despite a success rate of 99.26 percent for not producing crucial defects, more than \$28 million in market failure costs resulted! The cost of market failures due to serious defects was:

$$(.0295) \text{ sd/bottle} \times (500,000,000) \text{ bottles/yr} \times (\$0.47) \text{ cost/sd}$$
$$= \$6,932,500$$

The total market failure (MF) cost for year one was therefore:

$$\$28,305,000 + \$6,932,500 = \$35,237,500$$

Basis for Disposition Decision for Production Containing Defects

Before proceeding further, this is a good point to stop and review JEBB's basis for shipping production containing 0.74 percent crucial de-

TABLE 7-1. Defect Summary for A-1

	Crucial defects (%)	Serious defects (%)
Loose caps	.15	—
Tight caps	.25	.80
Lubricant in product	.15	—
Low-filled bottles	—	.40
Sticky bottles	—	.60
Foreign material in product	.09	.45
Label flaws	—	.30
Miscellaneous	.10	.40
Total	.74	2.95

fects and 2.95 percent serious defects into the market. When defects are detected in packaged product via product appraisals, the manufacturer has the option of shipping the product "as is," culling out the defective units by an inspection procedure, or scrapping the product. The decision is often based solely on the economics relating to the particular situation. Let's now review the pertinent economics for the JEBB Company during year one.

Assume that the average cost of an inspector, including overhead and benefits, was $12.50 per hour ($26,000 annually). Assume further that an average inspector could efficiently evaluate 180 bottles in 1 hour. This figures out to be an inspection cost of $0.0694 per bottle $\frac{\$12.50 \text{ cost/hr}}{(180) \text{ bottles/hr}}$. Each day JEBB planned to produce 2 million bottles $\frac{(500,000,000) \text{ bottles/yr}}{(250) \text{ days/yr}}$. Therefore, the cost to inspect one day's production would have been given by:

($0.0694) cost/bottle × (2,000,000) bottles/day = $138,800 cost/day

The average crucial defect level was 0.74 percent which corresponds to 14,800 crucial defects in the 2 million bottles of daily production. To scrap these 14,800 bottles of product at the $0.20 per bottle manufactured value after they had been culled from production would have cost an additional $2960. So the total cost to inspect one day's production so as to cull out the crucial defects would have been $141,760.

It was previously determined that the average market failure cost for a unit of this product with a crucial defect was $7.65. Thus, the market failure cost associated with shipping the 2 million bottles of production (1 day's) "as is" would be given by:

$$(14,800) \text{ cd/day} \times (\$7.65) \text{ cost/cd} = \$113,220$$

The cost to scrap 2 million bottles at the manufactured cost for 1 day's production would be given by:

$$(\$0.20) \text{ cost/bottle} \times (2,000,000) \text{ bottles/day} = \$400,000$$

The cost of physically scrapping the product would have to be added to this figure.

In net, it can be seen by comparing these costs that (a) the scrapping of a day's production is economically prohibitive (\$400,000); (b) the culling of defective units is not justifiable even with the horrendous crucial defect level of 0.74 percent (\$141,760); and (c) the "best" option is the loss of \$113,220 by shipping the product "as is." Actually, if you take the time to wade through the math, you will discover that in JEBB's situation, for any crucial defect level less than 0.93 percent shipping "as is" is the best economic alternative. At the 0.93 percent crucial defect level, the cost of culling the defective units is exactly equal to the cost of shipping "as is." Therefore, in the case studies for any segment of production containing a 0.93 percent or less crucial defect level, neither the culling of defectives by inspection nor the scrapping of the production will be considered. In a more general sense, attaining product quality by culling defective units is almost always an expensive alternative.

Actually, the only time during the course of the case studies that the crucial defect level exceeds 0.93 percent is when crucially defective bulk product is packaged into bottles. For this circumstance, 100 percent of the units possess a crucial defect. Again considering one day's production: (a) the cost to scrap would still be \$400,000 (plus scrapping costs); (b) the cost to ship "as is" would be \$15,300,000 (2,000,000 cd × \$7.65/cd); and (c) the cost to salvage would depend on the specific situation, but for almost all conceivable circumstances the cost of salvaging would exceed the \$400,000 scrapping cost. (The bottles would have to be individually emptied and individually cleansed; the product would have to be reprocessed and refilled into bottles.) Therefore, for this situation in the case studies, scrapping of the product is the least costly option.

The Total Quality Cost

Table 7-2 summarizes year one, rounding to the nearest \$1000.

JEBB expected \$50 million in profits annually (500,000,000 bottles/yr × \$0.10 profit/bottle). This profit level was premised on the absorption of

TABLE 7-2.   Cost Summary for A-1

P	= $	72,000 (P_T = $70,000; P_C= $2,000)
A	=	60,000
IF	=	5,303,000
MF	=	35,237,000
T	=	$40,672,000

negligible quality failure costs. Yet, during year one $40,540,000, over 80 percent, of these expected profits were lost owing to quality failures. A portion of these failure costs may not become apparent in the form of decreased profits until year two. However, the cause was unquestionably product quality during year one. Regardless, the point is that *more than $40 million of profit was lost due to inferior product quality*.

The Importance of Quality During a Market Introduction

Attention will now be focused on an even worse consequence. Recall the prior market research data. It showed that independent of the number of defects previously experienced, 33 percent of consumers will not re-purchase the brand for 1 year after purchasing a crucial defect and 2 percent will not repurchase the brand for 1 year after buying a serious defect. At JEBB's annual production rate of 500 million bottles, their crucial defect rate of 0.74 percent and serious defect rate of 2.95 percent resulted in the shipment of 3.7 million crucial defects and 14.75 million serious defects during year one. This means that during year one 1,516,000 potential users (.33 × 3,700,000 + .02 × 14,750,000) decided not to repurchase the new soft drink for at least 1 year. JEBB's market-ing forecast anticipated only 2.4 million users of the new product. Sixty-three percent of the expected market were "turned off"!

From a different perspective, remember that the average user was expected to purchase 208 bottles each year. Using this figure in conjunc-tion with the first-year defect rates demonstrates that the following prob-abilities existed for each one of the 2.4 million expected product users: (a) a 78.5 percent chance of purchasing at least one unit with a crucial defect: (b) a 99.8 percent chance of purchasing at least one unit with a serious defect; and (c) a 99.96 percent chance of buying at least one unit with either a crucial or a serious defect. This means that during year one, of the expected 2.4 million product users: (a) 1,884,000 obtained at least one crucial defect; (b) 2,395,000 obtained at least one serious de-fect; and (c) *only 960 did not purchase a unit with a defect*!

Much of this discussion has been based on market research data hopefully obtained from a normal distribution of product users. The results depicted the *average consumer. However, during a new brand or new product introduction, the user is not an average consumer.* Most of the users are *critical consumers* who are carefully evaluating whether they like or dislike the product. To a large extent, this decision will be based on how well the product fulfills their needs and expectations. To permit critical consumers to make this judgment with units which are inferior to the intended product can significantly enhance the probability that the user will not be satisfied with the new product. A consumer who is dissatisfied with a new product may decide never to repurchase it. An average consumer who obtains a defective unit of a brand with which he or she is familiar is more likely to react in a milder manner. This is because it is known that the product in its intended form does satisfy the consumer's needs and expectations. For the new brand, the critical consumer can easily conclude that the defective unit is characteristic of normal production, since there is no base for comparison. The point of this discussion is simply that *when a new brand or product is introduced into the market, the control of product variability is substantially more critical to long-term profits than at any other time in the product's life.* (This is not meant to infer that the control of product variability is unimportant at any time.)

Therefore, JEBB's new soft drink is probably in even more of a catastrophic state than described, where, based on the behavior of average consumers, it was concluded that JEBB had lost 63 percent of its potential users for at least 1 year. Probably JEBB had lost significantly more than 63 percent of its potential users for significantly longer than a year. A miracle would be required for this brand to survive. *A potentially very good product and all of the profit it could have accumulated have been forfeited because of the failure to control product variability.*

The Effect of Neglecting Intangible Market Failure Costs

Tangible market failure costs involve an actual monetary expenditure. Examples include the cost of warranty repairs or of a law suit due to faulty product quality. *Intangible market failures* are represented by lost sales and the related profits due to faulty product quality. Intangible market failure costs do not involve an actual cash outlay. However, in real money, $1 lost through intangible market failures is every bit as costly as any $1 cash outlay for tangible market failure costs. Because intangible market failure costs do not involve an actual cash flow and do not appear routinely in any formal cost report, it is possible for general management and even quality management to lose sight of this very important item.

To illustrate how easily this can happen, let's return to the case study.

JEBB's management could have developed a false sense of security in the knowledge that 99.26 percent of their production was free of crucial defects. Yet, despite this "high" success rate, 1,221,000 potential consumers (.33 lost consumers/cd of 3,700,000 cd), representing $25,396,800 in lost profit, decided not to repurchase the brand for at least 1 year because they purchased a unit with a crucial defect! Based only on my own limited knowledge, there may be a substantial number of companies of all sizes who operate without reasonable knowledge of the magnitude of their intangible market failure costs. However, our intent is not really to speculate as to the frequency with which this circumstance occurs. Rather, our intent is to discuss the possible consequence when it does happen.

In Chapter 6, we determined for JEBB the average market failure costs per occurrence for crucial, $\overline{MF}_{cd}$, and for serious, $\overline{MF}_{sd}$, defects. These were $7.65 per crucial defect and $0.47 per serious defect. If JEBB's management was incognizant of the importance of intangible market failure costs, they would have neglected to include the cost of business lost for quality reasons in the determination of $\overline{MF}_{cd}$ and $\overline{MF}_{sd}$. Doing this, $\overline{MF}_{cd}$ figures to be $0.78 per crucial defect, and $\overline{MF}_{sd}$ figures to be $0.06 per serious defect. The total market failure cost then figures to be:

$$\overline{MF} = (\$0.78) \text{ cost/cd} \times (3,700,000)\text{cd} + (\$0.06) \text{ cost/sd} \times (14,750,000)\text{sd}$$

$$\overline{MF} = \$3,771,000$$

Table 7-3 compares the actual cost picture with that portrayed if intangible market failure costs had been neglected or overlooked.

For the "actual case" it may be too late to save the brand. However, an analysis of the data leaves virtually no doubt that the lack of control of product variability was responsible for the horrendous loss of profit dur-

TABLE 7-3. Cost Summary for A-1 Showing Potential Distortion When Intangible MF Are Neglected

	Actual case	If intangible market failure costs are not included
P	$ 72,000	$ 72,000
A	60,000	60,000
IF	5,303,000	5,303,000
MF	35,237,000	3,771,000
T or T'	$40,672,000 (T)	$9,206,000 (T')

ing year one and, even worse, dealt the fatal blow to the new soft drink. At this point, appropriate action can be taken to prevent a similar occurrence for the next new or improved product. On the other hand, consider the quality cost figures for the situation if intangible market failures had not been considered for whatever the reason. From a review of the data, management could conclude that out-of-control product variability did result in significant extra costs. However, the reason for the new product's death is not readily evident. The potential devastating consequence is that, by not being able to pinpoint the true reason for the brand's demise, JEBB may repeat this unfortunate scenario for their next new product.

Use a "Best Estimate" When Data Are Lacking

This example clearly *demonstrates the distorted picture and the potentially disastrous consequences which can result from omission of a part of the total quality cost analysis.* This is true during either the development or the production phase of a product's life. Therefore, when needed data or information are not available, the *use of a "best estimate" is highly recommended.* To illustrate the value of a reasonable estimate, we'll return to the situation just described in which intangible market failure costs were neglected. Suppose, instead, that JEBB was fully cognizant of the importance of knowing the magnitude of intangible market failure costs. However, the market research data needed to include this item in the cost analysis were not available. Previously, this market research was assumed to show that 33 percent and 2 percent of the time the purchaser of a unit with a crucial and a serious defect, respectively, ceased buying the brand. Without these data, a decent estimate was needed so that $\overline{\text{MF}}_{cd}$ and $\overline{\text{MF}}_{sd}$ could be determined. Any estimate which was higher than the actual (33 percent and 2 percent) would have portrayed market failure costs in an even worse role than the catastrophic one they deserved. Consequently, management would readily have been able to identify the "bad actor." On the other hand, suppose that JEBB's estimates were low by a factor of three. That is, they estimated that only 11 percent and .67 percent of the time the purchaser of a unit with a crucial and a serious defect, respectively, ceased buying the product. Using these estimates, $\overline{\text{MF}}_{cd}$ = \$3.07 per cd and $\overline{\text{MF}}_{sd}$ = \$0.20 per sd. JEBB's "box score" is then illustrated in Table 7-4.

In net, *JEBB would be able to identify the true problem using an estimated value which fell anywhere in the range from at least three-fold lower than actual to infinitely higher than actual!*

TABLE 7-4. A-1 Cost Summary Using Estimates Instead of Market Research Data for Consumer Reactions to Defects

P	= $	72.000
A	=	60,000
IF	=	5,303,000
MF	=	14,309,000
T	=	$19,744,000

SUMMARY

This chapter contained some of the most important points in the book. An extreme case of poor quality was presented and discussed so that these key points would be more readily discernible. They are applicable to most consumer and industrial products. This is demonstrated in Chapter 11. Excessive product variability can result in the forfeiture of very large profits, and in the worst situation, it can be fatal to a product. When this occurs, all of the anticipated long-term profits are defaulted. A product is more vulnerable to these devastating consequences during its market introduction than at any other time during its life. For this reason, maximum efforts should be made during a product's development phase so that the total quality cost will be approximately optimized before manufacturing operations commence. It should be clear that one of the most important aspects in optimizing the total quality cost is the control of intangible market failure costs. These costs primarily represent lost business due to consumer dissatisfaction with product quality. To ensure that this aspect is adequately controlled requires a reasonable estimate of the rate at which failures will be shipped to the trade and the cost to the company of each failure which enters the market. When needed data or information are not available, the use of a judicious estimate is usually sufficient until better information becomes available.

Because failure rates are usually expressed as very small fractions, they are sometimes viewed as being inconsequential, and their effect is ignored. However, Case A clearly demonstrated that what may appear to be a relatively low failure rate can generate an enormous intangible market failure cost. Therefore, to neglect for any reason to consider the magnitude of intangible market failure costs is to incur a substantial risk that sizable profits will be needlessly lost year after year for the product's entire life cycle. In net, a competent and comprehensive optimization of the total quality cost *prior* to the start of production greatly enhances the probability that the quality function will make its expected contribution to profits.

Case B: A More Typical Situation

For Case B, JEBB was fully aware of the importance of quality relative to profits. Management was willing to commit whatever resources were required in order to attain control of product variability. However, JEBB did not utilize a well-organized and thorough management approach to develop an effective quality system prior to start-up. Let's now examine the details for Case B.

YEAR ONE (B-1) IN RETROSPECT

Test Run

Exactly as for Case A, JEBB incurred temporary preventive costs of $30,000 for assisting in the design of manufacturing operations, $30,000 to develop Component Specifications and the related inspection techniques, and $10,000 to develop finished product specifications and tests. They intended to spend $2000 in continuing preventive costs to identify each case of product by production day.

In this case, JEBB was quite cognizant of the potential dire effects which could result from a significant number of market failures, particularly during the market introduction of the new product. Consequently, they invested $40,000 in temporary preventive measures to conduct a test run of the manufacturing system. This was done at the earliest practical date so as to maximize the amount of time available to implement desired corrective actions before start-up. The results from the packaging portion of the manufacturing operation were identical to those actually experienced during year one of Case A: the crucial defect rate was 0.74 percent and the serious defect rate was 2.95 percent. Most of these defects were caused by problems associated with the capper, the bottle

filler, foreign material in the product, label flaws, and miscellaneous occurrences. Because only a few batches of product were mixed during the
test run, the only bulk product problem which became apparent was that
the scale used to weigh the flavor did tend to give spurious readings. The
cost of this failure was predicted to be $800,000 annually just as actually
occurred for Case A-1. JEBB used the failure rate data which was obtained from the test run to predict the magnitude of internal and market
failure costs for actual production of the soft drink. Table 8-1 summarizes
the predictions.

The results are very similar to the quality cost summary actually experienced for Case A-1. The main differences are the $40,000 spent to con-
duct a test run and that $4,503,000 in internal failure costs were not de-
tected, because only a limited number of bulk batches were processed.
Even so, an analysis of the total quality cost predicted for B-1 from the test
run leaves absolutely no doubt that a performance of this kind would be
unacceptable in that it would reduce the anticipated profit level very substantially.

Prevention Costs

In a responsible manner, JEBB then enacted the following additional
preventive measures to ensure substantially reduced failure rates when
production commenced:

1. In order to determine the source of the capper problem, $20,000 in
temporary preventive costs was allocated for a study. From this study
an additional temporary preventive cost of $5000 was incurred to
make relatively minor mechanical changes to the capper. It was also
deemed necessary to assign part of a mechanic's time to checking the
capper at regular intervals during production to be certain that it was
operating in the expected manner. This continuing preventive cost
(P_C) was $10,000 annually.

TABLE 8-1.   Predicted Quality Cost Summary for B-1 Based on Test-Run Results

P	= $	112,000 (P_T = $110,000; P_C = $2000)
A	=	60,000
IF	=	800,000
MF	=	35,237,500
T	=	$36,209,500

2. A similar study was made to determine the cause of the lubricant in the product. It was found that drops of oil were occasionally leaking from the top of the filler and flowing down the sides of the filling nozzles into bottles. For the study and to make the minor modifications, P_T expenditures were respectively $10,000 and $5000. Also, as with the capper, it was considered necessary to have a mechanic check the filler for proper operation at frequent intervals. For this, P_C was $10,000 yearly.

3. In addition to the actual failures which were discovered during the test run, the trial was also quite valuable in pinpointing a number of miscellaneous potential sources of failure costs. In order to prevent these potential problem areas from blossoming into real ones, JEBB spent $75,000 in P_T. An additional expenditure of $25,000 in P_C type costs was also allocated for this purpose.

4. Based on the initial test-run results, JEBB recognized the potentially horrendous failure costs which could result if a segment of production had to be recalled from the market. Since their planned shipping system would not be capable of locating a given production segment, JEBB would have had to recall every bottle from retail stores and from homes. To prevent this potential catastrophic event, JEBB decided to operate a product traceability system at a P_C of $50,000 annually. With this system they would be able to locate and identify any given segment of production at a manageable cost.

5. JEBB also recognized that when a quality problem occurred which was restricted to one packing line and/or only a few hours of production, it would be very expensive to scrap an entire day's production just because the represented production couldn't be located. Consequently, JEBB decided to code every case of product so that the packing line used and the hour of packing could be identified. The continuing preventive cost was $13,000 yearly rather than the $2000 of P_C to code the cases by the day of production.

JEBB's total preventive cost (P) was $333,000. This included a P_T of $225,000 and a P_C of $108,000.

Appraisal Costs

To appraise components and product, JEBB employed eight inspectors. These inspectors could also perform the required chemical and physical product tests. At $25,000 per year for each inspector, the cost was $200,000 yearly. With these eight inspectors JEBB expected: (a) 60 percent of the components would be inspected prior to use, (b) every hour one case would be inspected from each packing line; the intent was to detect a quality problem rapidly so that corrective action(s) could be enacted before the failure cost proliferated, and (c) all batches of product would be determined to be acceptable chemically and physically before being released for bottle filling; although four other batches would be mixed in the interim between batch mixing and its release for packing, a bulk product problem would be discovered before the cost of packaging materials became involved. The cost of destructive testing related to all of these inspections was $25,000 annually.

Other appraisal measures included:

1. A scale calibration program costing $10,000 annually was initiated based on the test-run result for the scale used to weigh flavor. The purpose of this program was to ensure the accuracy and precision of all scales at regular intervals.

2. To better assure that consumers did not obtain in-transit or insidious defects, JEBB spent $10,000 to appraise the quality of their product as it appeared in grocery stores.

3. JEBB spent $40,000 for market research on the new soft drink. This was done to confirm the data borrowed from a similar brand regarding the probability of consumer reactions after purchasing a unit with a crucial or a serious defect.

4. JEBB spent $10,000 to conduct a component supplier surveillance program.

The total cost for appraisals was $295,000.

Internal Failure Costs

When actual manufacturing operations began, internal failures occurred basically at the same rate as in Case A-1. However, they were detected sooner because of the more efficient appraisal system. In addition, the introduction of the scale calibration program twice prevented the production during the year of weakly flavored product and, hence, the associated failure costs which were present during A-1. Following is a summary of the internal failure costs which did occur during year one:

1. Each of the four times that chlorine remained throughout the system after a sterilization, the problem was detected in the first bulk batch of product before it was packed. At the time of detection, four additional

bulk batches had already been mixed. All five bulk batches contained chlorine and had to be scrapped at a cost of:

$$(5) \frac{\text{batches}}{\text{occurrence}} (150,000) \frac{\text{lbs}}{\text{batch}} \frac{(\$0.10)}{(.75 \text{ lb})} \times (4) \text{ occurrences} = \$400,000$$

In addition, the entire operation had to be shut down for 8 hours at each occurrence in order to clean the residual chlorine from the system. This cost was $1000 each time, or $4000. Therefore, the overall cost was $404,000 for year one.

2. On 3 of the 5 days when the incoming water supply was unacceptable, it was detected via component inspection prior to use. The entire operation was immediately shut down for the entire day. The cost was $3000 per day, or $9000. On the other 2 days, just as for the residual chlorine situation, the problem was discovered in the first bulk batch prior to packing. Four other bulk batches had already been mixed. All five batches had to be scrapped. The cost was $100,000 each time, or $200,000. Also, the operation was shut down for the day as soon as the problem was detected. This cost was $6000. The overall cost was $215,000 for year one.

3. Three of the five bottle receipts which contained grease were discovered prior to use via the component inspection plan. The bottles were rejected and returned to the supplier at no cost to JEBB. The other two receipts which contained grease were not inspected until after the bottles were used in production. The resulting product was discolored and potentially unsafe. The problem was detected by the packing line inspectors 1 hour after the bottles began to be used on all four lines. Because each case of product was identified by the hour it was packed, the represented production could be located and isolated. The bottle supplier agreed to absorb 50 percent of the scrapping cost. JEBB's cost was:

$$\frac{1}{2} \times [(\$400,000) \text{ value}/(96) \text{ hr} \times (4) \text{ hr/occurrence} \times (2) \text{ occurrences}]$$
$$= \$16,667$$

4. Only $200,000 in miscellaneous internal failures occurred. The reduction from the $500,000 experienced in Case A-1 was due to the expenditure of $100,000 for preventive measures to decrease miscellaneous failures.

The total for internal failure costs was $835,667.

TABLE 8-2.   Defect Summary for B-1

	Crucial defects (%)	Serious defects (%)
Loose caps	.04	—
Tight caps	.08	.40
Oil in product	.04	—
Low-filled bottles	—	.20
Sticky bottles	—	.20
Foreign material in product	.05	.20
Label flaws	—	.05
Miscellaneous	.04	.05
Total	0.25	1.10

Market Failure Costs

JEBB's trial run results showed decisively that emphasis had to be placed on eliminating sources of potential market failure costs before start-up. For Case B-1, JEBB's efforts between the test run and start-up did culminate in a substantial overall reduction in market failures as shown by Table 8-2.

The preventive measures instituted in the interim between the trial run and the start-up were responsible for the significant reductions in defectives caused by the capper, by the filler, and from miscellaneous sources. The decrease in foreign material in product was due mainly to the significant increase in the number of component receipts which were examined before use. Some of the cap and bottle receipts which contained foreign matter that could have entered the product were detected and rejected. The significant decrease in label flaws was also due to the more efficient appraisal of components prior to use. The cost of crucial defects was:

$$(.0025)\, cd/bottle \times (500,000,000)\, bottles/yr \times (\$7.65)\, cost/cd = \$9,562,500$$

The cost of serious defects was:

$$(.011)\, sd/bottle \times (500,000,000)\, bottles/yr \times (\$0.47)\, cost/sd$$
$$= \$2,585,000$$

The total market failure cost was $12,147,500.

The Total Quality Cost

Table 8-3 is a summary for Case B, year one (B-1) with figures rounded to the nearest $1000. For comparative purposes, the corresponding figures for Case A are also presented.

The Value of Preventive and Appraisal Measures

The key points and the lessons learned from Case A-1 are again evident in Case B-1. Case A represented an extreme, whereas Case B-1 represented a more typical result. In addition, it is very important to note that, in Case B-1, JEBB invested $496,000 more in preventive plus appraisal measures than in Case A. This incremental investment resulted in a $27,556,000 reduction in failure costs! It is in general true that *relatively small, prudent preventive and appraisal expenditures can result in relatively large benefits in the form of increased profits.*

The Value of Test Runs Before Start-Up

It is also important to note that the primary reason for JEBB being able to realize the enormous decrease in failure costs was because they were astute enough to appreciate the value of a test run. *We cannot overemphasize the utility and value of test runs.* Test runs provide data which enable the prediction of the magnitude of production failure costs and the identification of quality problem sources. Only with these types of information can corrective actions be planned and implemented so that when production actually begins, failure costs will be adequately controlled. In Case B-1 failure costs were not adequately controlled. However, the dramatic improvement relative to Case A-1 was achievable basically because a test run was performed. The test results clearly demonstrated

TABLE 8-3. Cost Summary for B-1

	Case B-1	Case A-1
P	$ 333,000	$ 72,000
A	295,000	60,000
P + A	628,000	132,000
IF	836,000	5,303,000
MF	12,148,000	35,237,000
T	$13,612,000	$40,672,000

that the proposed system for manufacturing the new soft drink would yield unacceptable failure costs during actual production. Consequently, additional actions were instituted *before start-up* to rectify the unacceptable situation. If it is not already evident, it will become so later in the book that follow-up test runs can also be very beneficial.

The timing for a test run relative to the scheduled start of production can be very important. The most accurate and comprehensive data are usually obtained when the test run is performed on the entire manufacturing system after it is assembled and in place. However, in order to conduct a test run of this kind, all of the unit operations must be ready for testing and be at a common location at a given time. In many, perhaps most, cases this circumstance will not take place until a time quite near the scheduled start-up. For these situations, little time is available between the test run and start-up for the manufacturer to solve the problems which the test run divulges and to incorporate corrective measures. Therefore, it is normally judicious to conduct test runs on each subsystem of the manufacturing operation at the earliest practical times and at convenient locations. In this manner, evaluative information can be available early, providing the time for implementation of desirable changes to prevent failure costs when actual operation commences. Then, when the entire system has been assembled in its intended location, a final test run(s) can be conducted to confirm that movement of the equipment did not cause any new·problem and to detect failures which might not have been detectable during the testing of subsystems; for example, failures which occur during the transfer of partially completed product from one unit operation to another one.

The Importance of Intangible Market Failure Costs on Quality

In Chapter 7 in the context of Case A-1, we discussed the badly distorted image of the quality system's contribution to profits which can result if intangible market failures are overlooked or ignored. If intangible market failure costs had not been included for any reason in Case B-1, the total failure cost would have appeared to be $2,141,000 and the total quality cost (T) would have appeared to be $2,769,000. In fact, these costs were $12,984,000 and $13,612,000 respectively. For the figures which did not include intangible market failure costs, JEBB's management could easily conclude the quality function contributed most of its potential to profits. They might also conclude that only a maximum of 4.3 percent profit increase, [($2,141,000) failure costs ÷ ($50,000,000) expected profits × (100)], was obtainable even if every failure cost was eliminated. In reality, failure costs are approximately $11 million a year higher, and a profit increase of 26.0 percent is potentially obtainable by eliminating these failure costs. By now it is obvious that *intangible market failure costs must be considered in order for any assessment of overall product quality to be valid.*

YEAR TWO (B-2) IN RETROSPECT

After reviewing the year-one quality cost summary which included intangible market failure costs, JEBB's management, not surprisingly, concluded that failure costs were exorbitant. This inferred that the total quality cost was far removed from its optimum value. Quality dedicated their year-two effort toward bring failure costs under control.

Prevention Costs

During year one, 48 percent of all crucial defects and 36 percent of all serious defects were caused during the capping operation. Accordingly, management assigned a small task force to study the capping operation with the objective of submitting a recommendation for significantly decreasing the failures. The temporary preventive cost (P_T) was $40,000. This included the cost to conduct experimental runs and the administrative costs for the task force. Their recommendations were that some rather extensive mechanical changes to the capper at a cost of $30,000 ($P_T$) were required, and that additional repetitive procedures for ensuring proper operation of the capper were needed at a cost of $20,000 yearly ($P_C$). The recommendations were accepted.

A similar approach was used to reduce the filler-caused defectives. For the task-force work, P_T was $30,000, and P_T to make the required alterations was $15,000. Additional procedures for ensuring correct operation were instituted at a P_C of $15,000 annually. Other preventive measures and the related costs were:

1. Management assigned one quality engineer full time to the new soft drink manufacturing system. The engineer's objective was to eliminate miscellaneous failures and any significant unanticipated failures which occurred. The cost of this engineer was $50,000 ($P_T$) for one year.

2. A P_T of $20,000 was needed to prevent the occurrence of residual chlorine remaining in the system after a sterilization. This included the costs to develop and confirm a standard procedure for flushing the system of chlorine and the costs to train operating personnel in the use of the procedure.

3. Purchase and use of an improved kind of nondurable filter for the water system was initiated. With the new filter, product with acceptable taste and clarity could be produced even for the 5 days when the incoming water supply was unacceptable. The cost of the improved filters was $25,000 per year ($P_C$).

4. All P_C's totaling $108,000 annually which were in effect during year one were continued, and all P_T's totaling $225,000 which were in effect during year one were not incurred again.

The preventive cost for year two was $353,000, with a P_T of $185,0000 and a P_C of $168,000.

Appraisal Costs

Appraisal measures introduced between the test run and the Case B-1 start-up to obtain improved control of foreign material in product accounted for a failure cost reduction of $1,728,000 per year. This was accomplished almost exclusively by increasing the frequency of appraising components prior to use from 20 percent to 60 percent. Realizing this, JEBB decided to increase its efficiency of appraising components before use from 60 percent to 100 percent. Four additional inspectors were hired at a cost of $100,000 per year. Also, JEBB hired two other inspectors at a total cost of $50,000 per year to ensure that all desired inspections and tests were performed on finished product before it was shipped to the market. Because of the addition of the six inspectors, destructive appraisal costs increased to $60,000 per year. Other appraisal measures were: .

1. JEBB increased its component supplier surveillance programs to supplement their new policy of assuring the quality of all components prior to use. During year two, $25,000 was required to implement this program.

2. With the introduction of many new operating procedures, a monthly operations audit program was initiated at a cost of $10,000 per year.

3. JEBB continued using (a) the eight inspectors already employed at $200,000 annually, (b) its scale calibration program at $10,000 annually, (c) its market survey at $10,000 annually, and (d) its market research program for consumer reaction to defects at $40,000 annually. JEBB repeated this study to be certain that it maintained a firm grasp on market failure costs.

The total cost of appraisals was $505,000.

TABLE 8-4.   Defect Summary for B-2

	Crucial defects (%)	Serious defects (%)
Loose caps	.003	—
Tight caps	.002	.04
Oil in product	.002	—
Low-filled bottles	—	.03
Sticky bottles	—	.02
Foreign material in product	.002	.03
Label flaws	—	.03
Miscellaneous	.003	.03
Total	.012	.18

Internal Failure Costs

Because of the timely preventive and appraisal measures which were instituted, internal failures were infrequent. A summary follows:

1. No costs were incurred owing to residual chlorine remaining in the system after a sterlization. As previously discussed, a procedure was initiated to avoid this circumstance.

2. No expenses resulted from unacceptable incoming water purity because of the use of the different type of filter which enabled the production of acceptable product for all incoming water conditions.

3. Continuation of the scale calibration program resulted in no failure costs owing to faulty scales.

4. No failure costs resulted from bottles containing grease. All bottle receipts were inspected before use and were rejected if they were unacceptable for use.

5. Only $100,000 in miscellaneous internal failures occurred. The reduction was mainly because of the assignment of the quality engineer to the project with this as his main objective.

The total internal failure cost was only $100,000.

Market Failure Costs

During year two, as discussed above, JEBB introduced a multitude and a variety of preventive and appraisal measures. Many of these were directed at eliminating, or significantly reducing, a particular market failure cost. The results of these efforts are given in Table 8-4.

The cost of the crucial defects was:

$(.00012)$ cd/bottle $\times$ (500,000,000) bottles/yr $\times$ ($7.65) cost/cd = \$459,000

The cost of the serious defects was:

$(.0018)$ sd/bottle $\times$ (500,000,000) bottles/yr $\times$ ($0.47) cost/sd = \$423,000

The total market failure cost was then \$882,000.

The Total Quality Cost

Table 8-5 is a summary for Case B, year two (B-2) with figures rounded to the nearest \$1000. For comparison, the corresponding B-1 figures are also shown:

The Value of Preventive and Appraisal Measures, Again

The total cost of quality was decreased greatly from \$13,612,000 during year one to \$1,840,000 during year two. This is a contribution to profits of \$11,772,000, and it is attainable every year. A more detailed analysis of Case B-2 reveals that of the failure cost reduction of \$12,002,000 for year two versus year one, \$9,719,000 (81 percent) was because of the introduction of preventive methodology at a one-time cost of \$185,000 and a continuing cost of \$60,000 per year. The remaining \$2,283,000 (19 percent) was because of increased appraisals costing \$210,000 annually. It is important to note that this enormous contribution to profits was achieved with a relatively small monetary investment in preventive and appraisal measures. The cost was only \$455,000 during year two and will

TABLE 8-5. Cost Summary for B-2

	Case B-2	Case B-1
P	$ 353,000	$ 333,000
A	505,000	295,000
P + A	858,000	628,000
IF	100,000	836,000
MF	882,000	12,148,000
T	$1,840,000	$13,612,000

be only $270,000 for every year thereafter to contribute $11,772,000 to profits every year. This represents 23.5 percent of the expected profit level. It is true, in general, that *very substantial contributions to profit can result from relatively small but prudent expenditures for prevention and appraisal techniques*.

Note the tremendous leverage (benefit for cost) which was obtainable through prevention alone. For preventive expenditures totaling $245,000 during year two, a cost savings of more than $10 million annually resulted. It will cost only $60,000 in future years to obtain the same savings. Preventive measures are intended to eliminate failure costs, whereas appraisals are normally utilized to detect quality problems sufficiently soon so that failure costs do not amplify out of control. This is not meant to imply that appraisal measures are of no value. From Case B-2 it is clearly visible that this is not so. However, prevention leads to problem elimination, while appraisal leads to problem reduction. Therefore, *prevention should be the primary weapon used to attack potential or real quality failure costs*.

Summary of Year Two

In net, because of the development of an effective quality system during year two, the total cost of quality was approximately optimized for that time period. However, what do you think the chances are of convincing the potential long-term users of the soft drink who were "turned off" by substandard product quality during year one to give the product another try?

SUBSEQUENT YEARS

In future years, JEBB's profits will benefit handsomely from the Quality System's very competent and effective efforts during year two. The Quality System's objective should be aimed at further progress of the total quality cost along the path to optimization. Only when proposed new preventive and appraisal measures cannot be justified based on the benefits they are expected to provide, and when no potential quality cost reduction opportunities remain to be investigated can JEBB, or any company, be reasonably confident that the optimum total quality cost has been approximated.

Optimizing the Total Quality Cost

For Case B, it is probable that following year two JEBB is not too far removed from its optimum total quality cost. The total quality cost for year two was $1,840,000. Of this amount $185,000 ($P_T$) was a one-time expenditure and will not be incurred in subsequent years. This results in a T of $1,655,000 each year. This is only 3.3 percent of the expected annual profits of $50 million and only 0.8 percent of the expected annual gross sales of $215 million. Since data of this type are usually regarded as confidential within a company, it is sometimes difficult to measure quality performance relative to competition. However, *when optimization of the total quality cost is competently and speedily managed until all potential significant cost reduction opportunities have been exhausted, there can be little doubt that the Quality System has approximated its maximum contribution to profits.* To control product variability does normally cost a substantial amount of money. For Case B, the cost will be about $1,655,000 every remaining year of the product's life. It should be clear by now, however, that the *failure to control product variability can be much more expensive and possibly catastrophic.*

SUMMARY

In review, Case B represented a more typical scenario illustrating the negative effect of poor product quality on profits. All of the major points for Case A were also apparent in Case B, only to a somewhat lesser extent. In addition, it was shown that to control product variability does require a significant cash outflow, but the failure to control product variability can be multifold times more expensive. Clearly, the best technique for controlling product variability was seen to be the utilization of equipment, procedures, and methodology which prevent failures. It was shown that the judicious implementation of preventive and appraisal measures can provide tremendous leverage in terms of the failure costs which they delete. That is, the introduction of relatively inexpensive preventive and appraisal measures can contribute very substantially to increased profits. The enormous value of conducting test runs of the proposed manufacturing system prior to start-up should have become obvious. From a trial of this sort, a prediction can be made as to whether failure costs will be adequately controlled during actual production. Most importantly, the sources of potential excessive failure costs can be identified so that appropriate corrective measures can be instituted before production commences.

Case C: "Overkill"

The attainment of product quality pervaded the entire JEBB organization for Case C. Starting at the top, management and workers were dedicated to the proposition that product variability had to be adequately controlled so that profit goals could be achieved. JEBB management thoroughly comprehended the special importance of controlling product variability during the critical time when a product was being introduced into the market. For these reasons, the attainment of product quality shared a dominant role with other cost-control goals from the day the new soft drink was conceived. Furthermore, general and quality management knew how to go about developing and maintaining an effective quality system.

YEAR ONE (C-1) IN RETROSPECT

Test Runs No. 1 and No. 2

Case C began exactly as did Case B. To review, the same initial preventive and appraisal measures were planned, and a test run (No. 1) was conducted. The results predicted a crucial defect rate of 0.74 percent, a serious defect rate of 2.95 percent, and the quality cost summary for year one (Table 9-1). This predicted performance was obviously deemed completely unacceptable. As in Case B-1, the same additional preventive and appraisal measures intended to greatly reduce failure costs were implemented. Cases C and B are identical until this point.

In Case C, however, because of their attitude toward quality and their expertise regarding the development of a quality system, JEBB's management insisted upon a follow-up test run to provide increased assurance of a successful introduction for the new soft drink. The test run

TABLE 9-1.   Predicted Cost Summary for C-1 from Test Run No. 1 Results

P	$ 112,000	(P_T = $110,000; P_C= $2000)
A	60,000	
IF	800,000	
MF	35,237,500	
T	$36,209,500	

(No. 2) cost $40,000 ($P_T$). The results estimated for year one a 0.25 percent crucial defect rate, a 1.10 percent serious defect rate, and a quality cost "box score" (Table 9-2). These results are essentially the same as for year one of Case B, with the exception that for Case C the preventive costs included an additional $40,000 for the second trial run. However, for Case B this summary reflected the *actual* quality costs for year one. A second test run was not performed. For Case C this summary represented only a *predicition* of year-one quality costs. No real damage had been done. Time remained to implement additional preventive and appraisal measures. For Case C, JEBB's management did indeed take actions prior to start-up. They viewed the estimated total quality cost of $13,652,000, more than 95 percent of which was due to failures, and the estimated yearly shipment of 1.25 million crucial defects and 5.5 million serious defects during the product's introduction as being absolutely intolerable.

Strategy for Developing a Quality System When Time Is Short

The time for the scheduled start of production is rapidly approaching. This can present a difficult dilemma. On the one hand, it is known that unless effective actions are swiftly implemented, failures will occur at an unacceptable level when production begins; yet, for some or many of these failures, the source of the problem is not clearly identifiable. On

TABLE 9-2.   Predicted Cost Summary for C-1 from Test Run No. 2 Results

P	$ 373,000	(P_T = $265,000; P_C= $108,000)
A	295,000	
IF	836,000	
MF	12,148,000	
T	$13,652,000	

the other hand, the start of production is on the immediate horizon. Several alternative approaches can be used to attack this dilemma. The strategy which I advocate in this circumstance, and which, therefore, is the one used in this case study, is to *introduce all practical preventive and appraisal measures which possess at least a reasonable chance of economically reducing the total failure cost*. If it later turns out that a measure of this type did not possess the needed ability, it should then be deleted.

The reason that I favor this tactic should become readily evident as we progress through this chapter. However, before proceeding, let's examine by way of an illustration this strategy versus another apparently logical one. Suppose that a manufacturer of sporting goods equipment plans to start production of a new tennis racket model in 3 weeks. The most recent trial run demonstrated that annual quality failures will be excessive. One of these failures is that the automatic equipment which applies the hand grip to the racket produces very loose or damaged grips at a predicted rate of $75,000 annually. A quality engineer was immediately assigned to perform an analysis of the cause of this particular failure and to recommend corrective action(s). After a few days the engineer concluded that the cause of the problem was either (a) the operator did not understand how to properly operate the equipment, or (b) the equipment itself required a number of specific refinements. To pinpoint which of these was the real cause could only be determined via prolonged operation of the equipment. To remedy the problem, the quality engineer recommended (a) a 1-week training seminar for all operators at a total cost of $4000, and/or (b) alterations to the equipment at a cost of $20,000. It was known that only one of these two expenditures would in reality be worthwhile. However, at this point in time the quality engineer was unable to identify which of the two was the valuable one. The strategy which I prefer would spend $24,000 to conduct the training seminar *and* to alter the equipment as recommended. Now let's examine another apparently attractive option: allocate the $4000 for the training seminar; then if the hand grip failures are still present when production commences, authorize the $20,000 for equipment modifications. Although this tactic may appear economically sound, it involves several distinct disadvantages. First, when all kinds of failures are considered for all unit operations, it is possible that a sizable number of situations like this one will be present. For each one a guess must be made as to the identity of the valuable measure(s). Obviously, owing to chance alone a number of these guesses will be wrong. This means that exactly at the time of manufacturing start-up, which is normally a very hectic time anyway, a goodly number of projects will have to be rapidly initiated and completed. Second, and most important, is the fact that when erroneous guesses occur, the production of some subquality product will take place. The critical importance of achieving outstanding product quality for the market introduction of a new or improved product was demonstrated in Chapter 7.

In this specific case, JEBB implemented all practical preventive and appraisal measures which appeared to exhibit any chance whatsoever of helping to ensure the control of failure costs when production commenced. They intended to evaluate the usefulness of these measures as time permitted and to weed out the worthless ones by the end of year one. Obviously, priority was assigned to the control of failure costs.

Appraisal Costs

Following is a list of the appraisal measures which were implemented:

1. The number of quality inspectors covering the three-shift operation was increased from eight to twenty-eight. Through this action it was expected that (a) all components would be inspected prior to use, (b) all bulk product would be tested before packing and before the next batch was completely mixed, (c) all finished product would be tested and inspected before shipment, (d) product from each packing line would be examined every 15 minutes to enable rapid detection of a problem, and (e) sufficient quality data would be available to guide the efforts of a four-engineer prevention team. The cost of the twenty extra inspectors was $500,000 per year. Also, $125,000 per year was the cost of the additional destructive testing.

2. A full-time operator-inspector was assigned to each packing line to visually observe each unit as it passed a given point on the line. Twelve inspectors were required for the four-line, three-shift operation. The cost was $300,000 per year.

3. The market survey program was expanded for an additional cost of $15,000.

4. An operations audit program costing $25,000 per year was initiated.

5. The scale calibration program was broadened at an aa..itional $40,000 per year cost.

6. The supplier surveillance program was amplified. The extra cost was $40,000 annually.

7. The market research study was expanded at an additional cost of $10,000 annually.

The cost of the additional appraisal measures was $1,055,000 per year. The total appraisal cost for year one was $1.35 million.

Prevention Costs

Following is a list of the preventive measures which were placed into effect in the interim between test run No. 2 and the start of production:

1. An additional \$20,000 (P_T) was spent to improve component specifications.

2. An additional \$20,000 (P_T) was expended to improve finished product testing methods.

3. A task force of four engineers was assigned to the start-up for the first year. The cost was \$200,000 (P_T). Their objective was to quickly attack and eliminated any unforeseen quality problems which appeared.

4. To further reduce capper-caused defects, an additional study team, further mechanical changes, and new operating procedures were used. The respective costs were \$40,000 (P_T), \$30,000 (P_T), and \$20,000 (P_C).

5. Similarly, to further decrease filler-caused defects, a new study team, additional mechanical changes, and new operating procedures were employed. The respective costs were \$30,000 (P_T), \$15,000 (P_T), and \$15,000 (P_C).

6. To provide insurance against homogeneous, bulk product problems such as the residual chlorine occurrence in Case B, a study team costing \$25,000 (P_T) implemented additional operating procedures costing \$100,000 (P_C) per year.

7. To provide further insurance against miscellaneous and potential problem areas, a study team costing an additional \$50,000 (P_T) instituted another \$100,000 (P_C) in operating procedures.

8. The component and product traceability system was improved at a cost of \$50,000 (P_C) each year.

Finally, JEBB conducted a third test run at a cost of \$40,000 (P_T). The purpose was to provide JEBB's management with complete confidence that failure costs would be under control during year one. The results closely approximated the actual year-one results, which are discussed later. Subsequent to test run No. 2, \$755,000 worth of year-one preventive measures were implemented. The total preventive cost for year one was \$1,128,000 with a P_T of \$735,000 and a P_C of \$393,000.

All of the preventive and appraisal measures which were instituted during Case C were also instituted during Case B. Many of these quality measures were actually introduced more efficiently in Case B. However, there is one very important difference which strongly favors the approach used for developing the quality system in Case C: For Case C, *all of the quality measures were placed into effect before the start of production for year one*. For Case B, many of these measures were introduced as late as during year two.

Internal Failure Costs

The cost of miscellaneous internal failures which occurred was $50,000. The modest reduction as compared to Case B-2 resulted from the additional operating procedures instituted versus miscellaneous failures and to the availability of the four-person prevention team. All other internal failures were prevented in the same manner as described for Case B-2. The total year-one internal failure cost was, therefore, $50,000.

Market Failure Costs

Quality inspection data showed the following incidence level for market failures (Table 9-3). The cost of crucial defects was $382,500, and the cost of serious defects was $352,000. The total market failure cost for year one was $735,000. The modest reduction relative to Case B-2 which is evident for market failure costs is due mainly to the availability of the four-engineer prevention team.

TABLE 9-3.   Defect Summary for C-1

	Crucial defects (%)	Serious defects (%)
Loose caps	.003	—
Tight caps	.002	.04
Oil in product	.002	—
Low-filled bottles	—	.03
Sticky bottles	—	.02
Foreign material in product	.002	.03
Label flaws	—	.01
Miscellaneous	.001	.02
Total	.010	.15

TABLE 9-4. Actual and Predicted from Test Run No. 3 Cost Summary for Case C-1

	Case C After Test Run No. 3 and Case C-1	Case C At Test Run No. 2 and Case B-1	Case B-2
P	$1,128,000	$ 333,000	$ 353,000
A	1,350,000	295,000	505,000
P+A	$2,478,000	$ 628,000	$ 858,000
IF	50,000	836,000	100,000
MF	735,000	12,148,000	882,000
(F)	(785,000)	(12,984,000)	(982,000)
T	$3,263,000	$13,612,000	$1,840,000

The Total Quality Cost

Table 9-4 is the quality cost summary for Case C, year one (C-1). For purposes of the discussion which follows, several other case bottom lines are also shown.

The Enormous Benefit of Test Runs

For C-1, the dramatic decrease in the total quality cost from what would have been $13,612,000 to $3,263,000 primarily resulted from the judicious use of follow-up test runs. Based on the results from test run No. 2, additional P&A measures were introduced. Test run No. 3 was performed to be certain that the new P&A measures did actually bring failure costs under control. The net effect was that year-one profits benefited by $10,349,000. The importance of test runs was discussed in Chapter 8, and the importance of follow-up test runs has been demonstrated in this chapter. To repeat, *the potential value of test runs can not be overstated.* Test runs do cost money, and they can sometimes be difficult to coordinate logistically. However, by comparing the total quality costs of $40,672,000 for Case A-1 (no test run), versus $13,612,000 for Case B-1 (one test run), versus $3,263,000 for Case C-1 (one test run, two follow-up test runs), it should be clear that the potential worth of test runs is enormous. The reason that the word "potential" is used is that in order to actually be useful, test run results must be appropriately acted upon. Stated from a different perspective, *the termination or omission of test runs until after at least one satisfactory test run has been achieved risks both short- and long-term profits.*

Exercise Caution When Developing a Quality System

The dramatic reduction in the total quality cost during the development of the quality system for C-1 was achieved despite a significant amount of inefficiency in the use of preventive and appraisal measures. The inefficiency was almost entirely owing to the ultraconservative approach adopted by JEBB when they realized that additional actions would have to be implemented in the short time period before start-up if product variability was to be adequately controlled. As evidence of this very conservative, inefficient use of P&A measures, see Table 9-4. Relative to Case B-1, Case C-1 employed an additional $1,850,000 in P&A measures to reduce failure costs by $12,199,000; Case B-2 employed only an additional $230,000 to reduce failure costs by $12,002,000. That is, 98 percent of the failure cost reduction obtained during C-1 was achieved during B-2 for only 12 percent of the P&A costs incurred during C-1. Clearly, many of the P&A measures employed during C-1 were ineffective. Despite this inefficiency, the total quality cost during C-1 was decreased by $10,349,000 relative to B-1! The point is that *when doubt exists for any reason*, such as lack of data, *concerning the value of a preventive or appraisal measure, it is usually financially wise to implement that measure at least until the doubt can be clarified*. Consider that, for most products, P&A costs are only a small fraction of expected profits, but the failure costs they avoid can be a very large fraction of expected profits. To illustrate, on the average, $1 of P&A expense reduced failure costs by $52.18 in proceeding from B-1 through B-2. The bottom line was that profits were increased by 24 percent of their expected level. Even when P&A costs were highly excessive, as in proceeding from C-1 at test run No. 2 through C-1 actual, each $1 of P&A-reduced failure costs by an average of $5.64. The bottom line was that profits were increased by 21 percent of their expected level. In net, *it is normally economically prudent to develp a quality system from a very cautious viewpoint*.

YEAR TWO (C-2) IN RETROSPECT

A Critical and Comprehensive Review of Year-One P&A Measures

Generally, JEBB was satisfied with year-one quality results. They decided not to introduce additional P&A measures during year two (C-2). However, JEBB knew before the start of production in year one that because of time constraints, they were applying "overkill" in order to ensure acceptable quality results. Therefore, JEBB critically reviewed the effectiveness of all quality measures employed during year one. Consequently, the following actions were initiated prior to year two:

Appraisal Costs

1. They deleted the use of all twelve operator-inspectors. Based on an examination of the number and types of defects eliminated by these inspectors, JEBB realized that at line speeds of 500 units per minute it was virtually impossible for the human eye to detect defective units as they passed the inspection point. This action reduced appraisal costs by $300,000 annually.

2. The number of quality inspectors covering the three-shift operation was decreased from twenty-eight to fourteen. Analysis of year-one data revealed that economic considerations favored appraising product every hour from each packing line rather than every 15 minutes as in year one. Furthermore, the extra data required to guide the efforts of the four-engineer prevention team were no longer needed. The elimination of fourteen inspectors saved $350,000 annually. In addition, destructive testing costs dropped by $75,000 due to the reduced inspection frequency.

3. It was determined that the scale calibration program was excessive. The program was revised, and the cost was thereby decreased by $25,000 each year.

Prevention, Internal Failure, and Market Failure Costs

Furthermore, of all the temporary preventive costs incurred in year one, a total of $735,000 vanished. Because each of these reductions was based on reliable data and information, and since no new P&A measures were introduced, internal failure costs and market failure costs remained the same as for year one.

The Total Quality Cost

The quality cost "box score" for year two (C-2) appeared as shown in Table 9-5. The total cost was decreased by $1,485,000 in proceeding from C-1 to C-2. This was accomplished by eliminating the one-time preventive costs and the obviously inefficient P&A measures from C-1. The total quality cost of $1,778,000 for year two is not greatly different from the $1,655,000 specualted during the discussion of year B-2 in Chapter 8 to be the approximate optimum total quality cost for JEBB's new soft drink. Basically, year two reinforces the main points in Case C-1. For the first 2 years of the new soft drink's market life, the estimated optimum quality cost was about $3,310,000 (2 × $1,655,000), and for Case C the actual 2 year combined quality cost was $5,041,000. The

TABLE 9-5. Cost Summary for C-2

	C-2	C-1
P_T	$ 0	$ 735,000
P_C	393,000	393,000
P	$ 393,000	$1,128,000
A	600,000	1,350,000
IF	50,000	50,000
MF	735,000	735,000
T	$1,778,000	$3,263,000

total quality cost for year one alone would have been $13,612,000 if the additional potentially valuable P&A measures had not been implemented based on *follow-up test run results.*

YEAR TEN (C-10) IN RETROSPECT

A Cost Savings Project

For the next 7 years, JEBB continued its quality program for year two and maintained a total quality cost which approximated the optimum value. This accomplishment assisted substantially toward JEBB's meeting its profit objectives over the time period. Year ten was the same as all of these years, including C-2, with one exception. A new quality engineer viewed the annual expense of $30,000 for quality operating procedures associated with the capper as being extravagant. Consequently, to save $10,000 per year, the engineer recommended deletion of one-third of these procedures. The personnel who had been involved in the start-up of the soft drink 10 years previously had changed, and no one could recall exactly why each of the quality procedures had been adopted. Since the engineer's line of reasoning seemed logical, the deletions were authorized.

Table 9-6 reviews the process which led to incorporation of the $30,000 for capper quality operating procedures: From Table 9-6, it is evident that the mechanical changes costing only $5000 and the quality procedures costing only $10,000 annually which were placed into effect between test runs No. 1 and No. 2 decreased capper-caused market failure costs by $11.65 million. Also, the mechanical changes costing only

$30,000 and the quality procedures costing only $20,000 annually which were instituted between test runs No. 2 and No. 3 reduced capper-caused market failures costs by $5,245,000. All of these actions were based on information and data gathered by a study team and confirmed by a test run. Since the results were very positive, it is probable that most of the actions were essential to the success experienced.

Quality Costs and the Total Quality Cost

For year ten, preventive costs were the same as for year two except that $10,000 ($P_C$) in capper quality procedures had been abandoned. The preventive costs totaled $383,000 ($P_T = 0$; $P_C = $383,000$). Appraisal costs were $600,000 and internal failure costs were $50,000, both identical to the year-two figures. Due to the reduction in capper quality procedures, the incidence level of capper-caused defects increased a small portion of the way back toward the level for test run No. 2. Capper-caused crucial defects increased to .02 percent and serious defects increased to .12 percent. (During test run No. 2, the figures were respectively 0.12 percent and 0.40 percent.) These increases altered the overall crucial defect level to .025 percent and the serious defect level to

TABLE 9-6. Summary of Actions to Decrease Capper Failure Costs for Case C

Actions initiated prior to the indicated test run	Case C, test run no. 1	Case C, test run no. 2	Case C, test run no. 3
P_T to determine corrective actions for capper-caused defects ($)	$0	$20,000	+$40,000
P_T to make capper mechanical changes ($)	$0	5,000	+ 30,000
P_C for capper quality procedures ($)	$0	10,000	+ 20,000
Defective level for the indicated test run	Case C, test run no. 1	Case C, test run no. 2	Case C, test run no. 3
Crucial defects (%)	.40	.12	.005
Serious defects (%)	.80	.40	.04
Market failure cost of defects based on indicated test-run results	Case C, test run no. 1	Case C, test run no. 2	Case C, test run no. 3
Crucial defects ($)	$15,300,000	$4,590,000	$191,000
Serious defects ($)	1,880,000	940,000	94,000
Total ($)	17,180,000	5,530,000	285,000

.23 percent. The total market failure cost for year ten was $1,497,000. The total quality cost summary for year ten (C-10) is given in Table 9-7.

The Erroneous Cancellation of a Valuable P&A Measure Can Be Quite Expensive

The intent during year ten was to save $10,000. Instead, the total quality cost increased by $752,000. In Chapter 8 we discussed the leverage effect: that an astutely selected P&A measure can frequently decrease failure costs by many times the cost of the measure. Unfortunately, the reverse is also true. *The inopportune deletion of a valuable P&A measure can increase failure costs many times greater than the cost savings anticipated from deletion of the P&A cost.* This is precisely what happen during C-10. The moral is that *existing P&A measures* should not be abandoned unless management is certain that the planned action will produce the desired objective. In C-2, fourteen quality inspector jobs and twelve operator inspector jobs were deleted based on a review of data from a full year (C-1) of operation and on a thorough economic evaluation. The planned annual savings of $650,000 was actually realized. In C-10, quality procedures associated with the capper were deleted based on no objections to the planned action. Data demonstrating the utility, or lack thereof, of these operating procedures were not analyzed, and the reason for initially incorporating these procedures was not fully researched.

The cancellation of existing P&A procedures basically involves a benefit versus risk analysis. For C-10, the potential benefit was an annual savings of $10,000. The risk turned out to be an annual loss of $752,000. In other words, seventy-five consecutive correct decisions to delete other

TABLE 9-7.   Cost Summary for Case C-10

	C-10	C-2 through C-9
P_T	$ 0	$ 0
P_C	383,000	393,000
P	$ 383,000	$ 393,000
A	600,000	600,000
IF	50,000	50,000
MF	1,497,000	735,000
T	$2,530,000	$1,778,000

similar P&A measures would be required in order to merely nullify the effect of this one erroneous decision! This is exactly the reason why a company must be absolutely sure before deciding to delete any P&A measures.

SUMMARY

In Case C, JEBB had an excellent attitude toward quality, and it possessed the know-how to develop and maintain a profitable quality system. JEBB conducted two test runs, both of which indicated that additional P&A measures were needed. When time became limiting, JEBB introduced all P&A measures which had any chance of economically reducing failure costs. They realized that many of these added measures would later prove to be worthless. A subsequent confirmatory test run showed that failure costs would be adequately controlled at start-up.

Case C demonstrated the extreme importance of continuing to conduct test runs at least until predicted quality failure costs are decreased to a level which can be tolerated when actual production commences. It also illustrated that caution should be highly visible during the development and management of a quality system. More specifically, whenever a doubt exists regarding the value of a P&A measure, it is usually profitable to implement or to continue use of that measure at least until the question can be resolved.

10 Case D: Optimum Design

As in Case C, JEBB's philosophy toward quality was characterized by an appreciation for the contribution to profits which outstanding product quality can deliver and the know-how to develop and maintain a profitable quality system.

YEAR ONE (D-1) IN RETROSPECT

Test Runs No. 1 and No. 2

This case began exactly as C-1. The same preventive and appraisal measures were introduced, and test run No. 1 was conducted. The results predicted a crucial defect rate of 0.74 percent, a serious defect rate of 2.95 percent, and a total quality cost of $36,209,500 for year one. Just as in C-1, JEBB viewed these results as intolerable and implemented additional preventive and appraisal measures. The results from the follow-up test run (No. 2) were the same as in Case C and predicted a crucial defect rate of 0.25 percent, a serious defect rate of 1.10 percent, and a total quality cost of $13,652,000 for year one. JEBB viewed these results as unacceptable. Cases C-1 and D-1 are identical to this point.

The Difference Between Cases C and D

For Case C-1, the time interval between test run No. 2 and the start of production was short. Therefore, all potentially valuable P&A measures were implemented prior to start-up. For case D-1, ample time was available between test run No. 2 and start-up to sort out those P&A measures which were really justifiable economically.

Quality Costs

The cost to distinguish between the valuable and the nonuseful P&A

137

measures was \$100,000 (P_T). Relative to C-1, the following P&A measures were determined to be not useful:

1. The additional \$20,000 (P_T) to further refine component specifications was not spent.

2. The additional \$20,000 (P_T) to improve finished product test methods was not spent.

3. The prevention task force of four engineers which was assigned to the start-up for the first year was ascertained to be lavish. Only one engineer was assigned, so P_T was reduced by \$150,000.

4. To provide insurance against homogeneous bulk product problems, the study team recommended only \$25,000 (P_C) of additional operating procedures rather than the \$100,000 (P_C) in C-1.

5. It was deemed unnecessary to provide further insurance against miscellaneous potential problem areas than the utility engineer assigned to the start-up. It was believed that he could rapidly attack this type of occurrence. Consequently, the study team costing a P_T of \$50,000 was not assembled, and the additional miscellaneous operating procedures costing \$100,000 (P_C) were not instituted.

6. The component and product traceability system was determined not to require improvement for \$50,000 (P_C).

7. It was shown that fourteen quality inspectors could adequately accomplish the required tasks. The additional fourteen quality inspectors, costing \$350,000 annually, were not employed.

8. It was determined that the twelve operator-inspectors, costing \$300,000 annually, would serve no useful purpose. The packaging line speed was too high to permit the efficient removal of defectives.

9. Because of the reductions mentioned in **7** and **8**, destructive testing costs were \$90,000 less than for C-1.

10. Other expenditures added during C-1 to improve existing appraisal technqiues which were not employed during D-1 were: \$15,000 for market surveys; \$15,000 for audits; \$40,000 for the scale calibration program; \$25,000 for the supplier visit schedule; and \$10,000 for market research.

The net effect was that only the worthwhile additional P&A measures remained at start-up. Since the only difference between Case D-1 and Case C-1 was that time allowed the deletion (nonintroduction) of useless P&A measures during D-1, failure costs were the same for both cases. Test run No. 3 yielded this information prior to start-up.

TABLE 10-1. Cost Summary for D-1

	A-1	B-1	C-1	D-1
P_T	$ 70,000	$ 225,000	$ 735,000	$ 595,000
P_C	2,000	108,000	393,000	168,000
P	$ 72,000	$ 333,000	$1,128,000	$ 763,000
A	60,000	295,000	1,350,000	505,000
IF	5,303,000	836,000	50,000	50,000
MF	35,237,000	12,148,000	735,000	735,000
T	$40,672,000	$13,612,000	$3,263,000	$2,053,000

The Total Quality Cost

The quality cost summary for Case D along with comparable figures for the other cases is given in Table 10-1.

Requisite Ingredients for Optimizing a Quality System Before Start-Up

The total quality cost of $2,053,000 for D-1 was significantly less than for year one of any other case. This was primarily because of JEBB's attitude toward and knowledge of product quality during Case D, and due to the implementation of only P&A measures which were known to be economically justifiable. Considering the amount of P_T employed during D-1, it is probable that the total quality cost for Case D-1 is approximately at the optimum value for year-one operation. The importance of approximating optimization of the total quality cost for year one has been emphasized in Cases A, B, and C. In order to have even a reasonable chance of accomplishing this, three fundamental ingredients must be present simultaneously:

1. A genuine belief that product quality is important must exist through the entire organization. The attitude manifested from this belief will provide the required motivational and cooperative effort.

2. Competent people who possess the necessary expertise must be available to manage and lead the optimization effort.

3. The *time* must be available to carry out an organized and thorough approach to quality cost optimization prior to the start of production.

Although the attainment of particularly **1** and **2** can tax management capability to its utmost, both are achievable if upper management is committed. However, for a whole host of reasons, most not relating to product quality, it is not often that sufficient time is available to permit optimization of the total quality cost prior to start-up. Therefore, a decision must be made as to the best way to manage the total quality cost during initial production until optimization can be accomplished. To do this, refer again to Table 10-1.

Case A-1 represented the extreme case of gross quality negligence. P&A methods were virtually nonexistent. The total quality cost exceeded the approximate year-one optimum value by $38,619,000. This represented 77 percent of expected profits. Even for the more typical case of B-1, which involved some degree of ineptitude in the quality function, the approximate year-one optimum cost was exceeded by $11,559,000. This represented 23 percent of expected profits. At the other end of the spectrum, Case C-1 represented the extreme case of vast overkill. P&A measures were established ridiculously in excess of what were actually needed. Even in this extreme situation, the total quality cost was only $1,210,000 greater than the approximate year-one optimum cost. This is only 2.4 percent of anticipated profits. The moral is that *when the total quality cost cannot be optimized before start-up, it is almost always astute to incorporate all potentially useful P& A measures.* Actually, this is just an application at a critical point in time of a lesson contained in Chapter 9.

YEAR TWO (D-2) IN RETROSPECT

The Total Quality Cost

The total quality cost was essentially optimized during year one. Therefore, during year two the only change was that all P_T was deleted. The "box score" is shown in Table 10-2.

TABLE 10-2.   Cost Summary for D-2

P_T	$ 0
P_C	168,000
P	$ 168,000
A	505,000
IF	50,000
MF	735,000
T	$1,458,000

The $1,458,000 is the approximate optimum total quality cost annually for JEBB's soft drink subsequent to year one. This amount represents 2.9 percent of anticipated annual profits and 0.7 percent of gross sales.

Possible Frustrations for Quality Function Personnel

In Case D, the people responsible for managing the quality system did an outstanding job. The total quality cost was optimized before production of the soft drink commenced. From the very outset, the quality system made its maximum contribution to profits and ensured that the product had an opportunity for a fair assessment by potential users. Nonetheless, the individuals responsible for the excellent result might not have received the reward or approbation that they richly deserved. This is because it is not unusual for businesses to view product quality from the negative perspective that product quality can only influence profits in a neutral or an adverse direction. In this situation, management and the quality function will probably agree to some fixed monetary (budgeted) amount for controlling a product's variability. Management will include this amount in their calculations to estimate the profits to be obtained from the sale of the product. Then, in the interim prior to start-up, either of two scenarios can occur:

1. It is ascertained via trial runs, or whatever, that additional funds are needed for P&A measures to eliminate quality failure costs. Management may view this as poor performance in the form of inadequate planning. They will be hard pressed to comprehend the benefit from authorizing the additionally requested money, since the budget allocation implied that failure costs would be negligible. However, they will have no difficulty comprehending that the extra costs will reduce the expected profit level.

2. The initial monetary allocation was sufficient to cover the needs of the quality function. It is unnecessary to request additional funds. Management will probably view this as what was expected.

When production begins, two other possible scenarios exist:

1. Excessive failure costs must be absorbed. Since this affects the expected profit level in a negative direction, it will probably be viewed as poor performance, and for most situations this will be correct.

2. Failure costs are nominal. The expected profit level is attained. Management might view this quality performance as exactly what was expected from the quality function, but no more: an acceptable but an average effort.

In other words, when product quality is viewed from a negative standpoint, the individuals responsible for quality results can find themselves in a "can't-win" circumstance. In the eyes of management, there may be no room for outstanding performance or contribution. This can lead to some very frustrating experiences for these individuals. Consequently, it becomes increasingly difficult to attract and to retain competent, professional people to assume responsibility for quality function results. This circumstance by itself can have a substantial negative impact on profits.

The Total Quality Cost Concept as a Potential Cure for this Frustration

I believe that the solution to this dilemma lies in the utilization of the total quality cost concept. This concept views the quality system's contribution to profits from a positive perspective. It also merges the objective of the business with the objective of the individuals responsible for product quality. The result is a single common goal: **the maximization of profits.**

From the standpoint of the business, the quality cost concept yields a more realistic estimate for the profit level to be expected, because *all* quality costs are included. Realistic profit estimates make realistic decisions possible. They also avoid the disappointment which originates with the setting of unattainable goals. Just as importantly, the use of this concept motivates the business to be highly receptive to the authorization of additional expenditures for attractive P&A measures. This is because the benefit of the expenditure to decrease the total quality cost and hence to embellish profits is readily visible.

From the standpoint of the people performing the quality function the total quality cost concept serves to document individual and group contributions to the company's success as manifested by profits. These contributions can be expressed in terms of the amount of increased profit generated and/or the speed with which the total quality cost is optimized.

In net, the total quality cost concept provides incentive for both the business and the individual to rapidly optimize the quality system's contribution to profits.

Effective use of the total quality cost concept requires the presence of the following ingredients:

1. An organized, comprehensive approach to the development and management of a quality system is necessary to ensure that all pertinent factors are included.

2. Competent quality system personnel who understand and believe in

the value of the concept must be employed to manage, lead, and perform the necessary tasks.

3. Upper management must be committed to the concept. Only then will needed resources be available, and will management want to swiftly initiate whatever actions are dictated from analysis of the total quality cost data.

The Total Quality Cost Concept Has Not Yet Attained Widespread Use

Although the total quality cost concept is not new, it does not appear to be broadly used by industry. In general, quality and upper management personnel have not been presented with the opportunity to become familiar with its value. The everyday needs and pressures involved in operating a profitable business make it unlikely that an educational effort of this nature will suddenly appear within businesses or industries. It may not even occur gradually in this manner. I believe that this educational process will most likely emanate in the college/university system. Beginning in about the middle 1960s consumers demonstrated an increased interest in and knowledge of the quality of the products which they purchased. Today, in the 1980s this consumer interest in and knowledge of product quality is even more intense. It appears to be spurred on by a combination of economic conditions; publicity surrouding incidents when subquality product penetrates the market place; the high level of visible regulatory activity in this arena (e.g., relative to product recalls); and the fact that, in today's sophisticated economy, the degree of excellence for most products is so high that the condtrol of product variability image which a company portrays can be an important element to consumers in choosing the brand of a particular product which they will buy. There is no reason to believe that the current level of consumer concern regarding product variability will subside at any time in the near future.

Will Colleges and Universities Provide the Educational Foundation?

As a consequence, many colleges and universities are beginning to include courses relating to the quality function in their engineering and business administration school curricula. In 1981, there were at least two universities which offered a bachelor of science degree in quality engineering. As this practice gains momentum and becomes more widespread, there will probably be a substantial number of bright and talented college graduates who will desire and seek jobs associated with the attainment of product quality. These people will provide the needed pool of competent and enthusiastic quality system personnel who understand and believe in the total quality cost concept. Furthermore, they will probably bring with them new "tools" which can facilitate use of the concept. These graduates will in turn educate their peers, subordinates and managers in the value and mechanics of this concept.

Regardless of the path by which it eventually takes place, in my opinion it is inevitable that the total quality cost philosphy, or its equivalent, will gain broad acceptance and use among industries which manufacture a product. The case studies and examples contained in this book have demonstrated conclusively that product quality can very substantially affect profits. Therefore, product quality must be considered an integral part of a business. For any important aspect of any business, how can responsible and profitable decisions be made without accurate assessments of the total financial effect of these decisions on the business? For product quality decisions, the change in the magnitude of the total quality cost provides the required information directly.

11 Traits of a Profitable Quality System

To develop and maintain a profitable quality system, management must know the key characteristics which are usually present in such a system. A valuable insight regarding these characteristics can be gained by reviewing, comparing, and consolidating the important lessons contained in the case studies with particular emphasis on the year-one results.

The Effect on Profits of Management's Attitude and Approach Toward Quality

Recall that for the case studies, the JEBB Company was a moderate-size developer, manufacturer, and marketer of soft drinks. JEBB had developed a new, sparkling clear, peppermint-flavored, carbonated beverage. A 0.6 percent share of the huge carbonated beverage market was predicted for the new product. This translated to expected annual sales of 500 million 12-ounce bottles. The manufactured cost of the new soft drink was $0.20 per bottle, and the anticipated profit margin was $0.10 per bottle sold. Each case study considered a different attitude toward product quality and/or a different approach to the development and management of a quality system for the new soft drink.

Case A

For Case A, JEBB did not regard the control of product variability as being important. Not surprisingly, product variability was highly excessive. The first-year result was a devastating loss of profit and a catastrophic loss in numbers of potential loyal customers. It is extremely doubtful that the soft drink could have survived this market introduction.

Case B

For Case B, the JEBB Company viewed the control of product variability as having prime importance. However, the quality system which they developed and utilized was neither sufficiently comprehensive nor deep to ensure that quality objectives would be met. The first-year result was the forfeiture of a large amount of profit and the loss of a very large number of potentially loyal customers. Subsequently, JEBB acquired the expertise and personnel to develop and manage an effective quality system. From year two on, the total cost of quality was approximately optimized. However, JEBB's real challenge during these years was to convince the multitude of potential loyal product users who were "turned off" due to substandard quality during year one to give the soft drink another chance.

Case C

In Case C, JEBB regarded product quality with the same high respect as in Case B. Additionally, they possessed the acumen to develop a comprehensive and deep quality system. However, insufficient time was available before start-up to resolve many questions regarding the real utility of many of the recommended P&A measures. Taking this into account, JEBB elected to pursue the conservative alternative of instituting all practical actions which had a chance of economically eliminating failure costs. The first-year result was exactly what JEBB anticipated: profits were near the expected value. However, JEBB sacrificed a relatively small percentage, although a significant monetary amount, of expected profits in order to avoid losing potential long-term loyal product users. Also, during year one, they identified and deleted the P&A measures which turned out to be of no real value. Starting with year two and continuing for the remaining life of the brand, the Quality System's contribution to profits was maximized.

Case D

For Case D, JEBB had the same respect for product quality and the ability to develop and manage an effective quality system as in Case C. Additionally, they had the luxury of the time to resolve the quality issues before start-up. The first-year result was that the total quality cost was optimized from the very start of production. Very few potential loyal, long-term customers were lost due to substandard product quality. In subsequent years, the Quality System continued to make its maximum contribution to profits.

To facilitate comparisons of the case studies, a cost summary which includes each year of each case discussed is presented in Table 11-1 on subsequent pages. Individual preventive and appraisal expenditures are itemized so as to capture the spirit of each of the quality systems employed. From the detailed discussion of these cases and from the cost summary, it is apparent that *both the attitude and approach of the business toward the control of product variability had an enormous effect on profits*.

The Lessons Contained in the Case Studies Apply to Most Manufactured Products

One might rightfully wonder if the lessons derived from the case studies have general application to most manufactured products. To address this concern, consider that *all of the conclusions which lead to these lessons were based on magnitudes of T*, the total quality cost, or *on magnitudes of Q*, the total quality cost expressed as a fraction of profits. These values of T and Q were determined for the complete spectrum of quality systems ranging from totally ineffective to very efficient, and they were based on a consumer product characterized by the key marketing parameters of a low unit manufactured cost ($0.20 per item) which permits a low retail price, a low unit profit margin ($0.10 per item), and a very high sales volume (500 million units per year). Relative to this product, a very high number of all marketed commodities exhibit a unit manufactured cost of the same order of magnitude or higher; a unit profit margin of the same order of magnitude or higher; and a sales volume of the same order of magnitude or lower. The following discussion analyzes the effect on T (or Q) of a shift in each of these marketing parameters in a direction so as to include most marketed products.

The Effect of a Higher Unit Manufacturing Cost

For products with the same unit profit margin, the same sales volume, the same quality failure rate (percentage of failures), and similar quality systems, *the effect of a higher unit manufactured cost is that T will remain constant or increase*. For many cases, an increased unit manufactured cost will not affect T. However, T will increase if, for example, destructive product testing constitutes a significant portion of the appraisal program or if a significant amount of production must be scrapped.

The Effect of a Higher Unit Profit Margin

For products with the same unit manufactured cost, the same sales volume, the same quality failure rate, and similar quality systems, *the effect of a higher unit profit margin is that T will remain constant or increase*. This is because each unit which is not purchased by dissatisfied customers represents an increased loss of profit. For a constant quality failure rate, the total market failure cost and, hence, T will increase. The only exception is the unlikely event when zero market failures are being manufactured. For this circumstance T will not change.

TABLE 11-1. Summary of Case Studies of JEBB Company

(Figures in thousands of $)	Product's death	Large, early profit loss			Overkill			Optimum	
	A-1	B-1	B-2	B-3	C-1	C-2	C-10	D-1	D-2
P_T									
Assist in the design of manufacturing operations	30	30	—	—	30	—	—	30	—
Develop Component Specifications	30	30	—	—	50	—	—	30	—
Develop FPS and test methods	10	10	—	—	30	—	—	10	—
Capper study	—	20	40	—	60	—	—	60	—
Capper mechanical changes	—	5	30	—	35	—	—	35	—
Filler study	—	10	30	—	40	—	—	40	—
Filler mechanical changes	—	5	15	—	20	—	—	20	—
Bulk product problems study	—	—	20	—	25	—	—	25	—
Sort out worthless prevention measures	—	—	—	—	—	—	—	100	—
Miscellaneous	—	75	—	—	125	—	—	75	—
Prevention team	—	—	50	—	200	—	—	50	—
Test runs	—	40	—	—	120	—	—	120	—
P_C									
Coding of product cases	2	13	13	13	13	13	13	13	13
Capper quality operating procedures	—	10	30	30	30	30	20	30	30
Filler quality operating procedures	—	10	25	25	25	25	25	25	25
Bulk product quality operating procedures	—	—	25	25	100	100	100	25	25
Traceability system operation	—	50	50	50	100	100	100	50	50
Miscellaneous quality operating procedures	—	25	25	25	125	125	125	25	25

A	350	350	350	350	700	350	350	200	50
Quality department inspections of components and product									
Operator inspections of product	—	—	—	—	300	—	—	25	—
Destructive testing	60	60	75	75	150	60	60	—	10
Audits	10	10	25	25	25	10	10	10	—
Component supplier surveillance program	25	25	50	50	50	25	25	10	—
Scale check and calibration program	10	10	25	25	50	10	10	10	—
Market research studies	40	40	50	50	50	40	40	40	—
Market surveys	10	10	25	25	25	10	10	10	—
cd (%)	.010	.010	.025	.010	.010	.012	.012	.250	.740
sd (%)	.15	.15	.23	.15	.15	.18	.18	1.10	2.95
P	168	763	383	393	1128	168	353	333	72
A	505	505	600	600	1350	505	505	295	60
P+A	673	1268	983	993	2478	673	858	628	132
IF	50	50	50	50	50	100	100	836	5303
MF	735	735	1497	735	735	882	882	12,148	35,237
F	785	785	1547	785	785	982	982	12,984	40,540
T¹	ND	ND	ND	ND	ND	ND	ND	2769	9206
T	1458	2053	2530	1778	3263	1840	1840	13,612	40,672

Note: ND means not determined.

The Effect of a Lower Sales Volume

For products with the same unit manufactured cost, the same unit profit margin, the same quality failure rate, and similar quality systems, *the effect of a lower sales volume is that Q will remain constant or increase*. To understand this, consider the mathematical definition of Q: $Q = \dfrac{T}{\text{profits}}$.

Firstly, realize that for products with the same unit profit margin, profits will decrease in direct porportion to a decrease in sales volume. That is, if product B's sales volume is 75 percent as high as product A's sales volume, product B's profits will also be 75 percent of product A's profits. Secondly, consider that $T = P + A + F$. For a constant quality failure rate, which we have assumed, failure costs decrease in direct proportion to the sales (or production) volume. This is also true for many P&A costs. However, there are other P&A costs which will be incurred regardless of the sales volume. Examples include the cost of a study team to decrease a 0.25 percent crucial defect level, the cost of a quality audit, and the cost of a scale and instrument calibration program. The effect of costs of this type is that T will not decrease as rapidly as a decrease in the sales volume. Therefore, $Q\left(\dfrac{T}{\text{profits}}\right)$ will be greater for products with lower sales volumes. To digress for a moment, note that as the sales volume continues to decrease, Q will continue to increase. In the extreme, when the sales volume is quite low, the situation characterizes a small business. In other words, *the control of product variability is even more important for small businesses than for large companies*.

   In net, starting with JEBB's new soft drink and proceeding in a direction so as to include most consumer and industrial products, any change in a pertinent product marketing parameter will cause T (or Q) to remain constant or to increase. Therefore, by examining and assimilating the key points from the JEBB case studies, the general traits which characterize profitable quality systems can be identified. Each of these traits will now be discussed.

TOP MANAGEMENT UNDERSTANDS THE RELATIONSHIP BETWEEN QUALITY AND PROFITS

First, *top management thoroughly understands that the control of product variability is very important to profits*. This is not only a trait, but is a prerequisite for a profitable quality system. Only when top management comprehends this fact, which was clearly demonstrated by the case studies, will the required financial and human resources be allocated so that an effective quality system can be developed and managed. Furthermore, when top management understands the importance of controlling product variability, they will ensure that this philosophy pervades the entire organization so as to serve as the foundation for a strong and healthy quality system.

THE QUALITY SYSTEM IS COMPREHENSIVE

Second, *a comprehensive program for the development and maintenance of the quality system* is utilized. To be comprehensive, a program must (a) include an examination of all manufacturing functions for needed P&A measures against anticipated failures; (b) include sufficient appraisals to ensure the speedy detection of unanticipated failures; and (c) consider the effect of all kinds of quality failures. Regarding (c), the case studies showed that the omission of a type of failure can yield a badly distorted, or even false, picture of a quality system's influence on a product's profitability. The case studies also showed that when information or data are lacking, the use of a reasonable estimate will usually be far superior to ignoring consideration of a type(s) of failure. This is especially true for intangible market failures which can be difficult to measure and to quantify. However, the case studies demonstrated that intangible market failures can dramatically influence a product's profitability.

In addition, a comprehensive quality system must utilize a common language for its various aspects and one which is related to company goals. This is necessary so that quality system decisions can be made based on valid assessments of alternatives, and so that these decisions will be consistent with business objectives. Money is the only language that I know of which will satisfy both criteria. To illustrate the need for this common denominator, consider a manufacturer of bicycles. The producer's quality data show that, on the average, internally detected defects are being generated at 5.0 percent. A breakdown shows that 4.0 percent are units with a drive chain which does not seat properly on the sprocket wheel; the other 1.0 percent are units with a deformed front wheel rim. Both defects prohibit normal riding of the bicycles. The manufacturer desires to eliminate both defects, but only has people resources to address one at a time. Therefore, the manufacturer must decide which defect to eliminate first. On the basis of the defect level, the drive chain would warrant first priority. However, if the labor cost to properly seat the drive chain is only $1 per unit, whereas the labor plus material cost to replace a bent rim is $20 per unit, a different picture emerges. For this situation per 100 bicycles produced, the internal failure cost to the manufacturer is $4 to rectify the drive chain defects, but $20 to rectify the bent rims. Obviously, the bent rims deserve higher priority. *A defect level by itself has little meaning. However, a defect cost can be related directly to profits.*

PREVENTION IS EMPHASIZED

Third, *the prevention of failure costs is emphasized*. Preventive actions eliminate real and potential failure costs, whereas appraisals only detect existing failure costs. In addition, many prevention costs are temporary,
while most appraisal costs are repetitive. (This is not meant to imply that
appraisal measures do not serve a useful purpose. In fact, appraisals are
the best means of controlling unanticipated failure costs.)

ALL PERSONNEL KNOW THE IMPORTANCE OF PRODUCT QUALITY, ESPECIALLY FOR A MARKET INTRODUCTION

The fourth trait of a profitable quality system is that *all personnel are
acutely aware of the extreme importance of controlling a product's variability during its market introduction*. A product's degree of excellence has been
established by the conclusion of its design. Before starting to construct
manufacturing facilities, the wise marketer will have conducted adequate testing to gain confidence that the product and its degree of excellence do, in fact, appeal to a sufficient number of consumers to be profitable in a market which usually includes formidable competition. The
marketing challenge is then to convince as many consumers as possible
to try a unit of the product. During this trial, the product will be subjected to a critical evaluation. Users who like the product will probably
repurchase it and/or other products manufactured by the marketer.
Users who do not like the product will probably not repurchase it, if it is
an inexpensive, nondurable product; or not repurchase other products
sold by the marketer, if it is an expensive, durable item. For every one of
these customers who would have found the product to be appealing but
who did not only because an initial unit of inferior quality was obtained,
all profit associated with the sale of that product over its entire lifetime to
that customer and/or profit from other products sold by that marketer to
that customer may have been defaulted. Since the user had never before
tried the product, he or she had no reason to believe that the initial unit
with inferior quality did not represent the product in its intended form
or in the form in which it was available. If this circumstance occurred for
very many consumers who would otherwise have liked the product, the
short- and long-term profit level for the product could be substantially
reduced. In the extreme, Case A showed that profits would be an-
nihilated, and the product would not survive in the market.

Contrast this situation with that of a long-time user of a product who
buys a unit of inferior quality. In this circumstance, due to familiarity
with the product in its intended and usual form, the user realizes that an
atypical unit has been purchased. Because the consumer alreadys knows
that he/she likes the product, the probability that this consumer will not

repurchase the product and/or other products sold by the producer is much lower than for a new product.

Therefore, *the challenge to a quality system during the market introduction of a brand is to provide product quality* (control of product variability) *superior to that which is needed* after the brand becomes established. This is completely consistent with the total quality cost concept. From this discussion, it is evident that the cost of the average market failure will almost always be at its maximum value during a product's introduction into the market.

Tools to Assist in Achieving Superior Quality at Start-Up

The attainment of superior control of product variability during the initial production phase of a product's life is contrary to the natural tendency for variability to decrease with time as the production "bugs" become "ironed out." However, it is quite clear that this is, in fact, what is required. It is fortunate that three basic "tools" exist for assisting to obviate this difficult requirement.

Competent Design

The competent design of the product and of manufacturing operations is a requisite. In Part II we discussed the key areas which must be effectively managed to have a successful quality system. By reviewing this discussion, we can see that a very high percentage of the work can be completed during a product's design phase before manufacturing operations commence. Thus, if the quality system is competently and efficiently developed, most of the needed people, equipment, procedures, and subsystems can be in place before start-up.

Test Runs

Test runs are very useful for ascertaining the effectiveness of design efforts without risking actual production and for predicting failure levels and failure costs for actual production. If the predicted failure costs are unacceptable, there is still time to institute appropriate action(s) before production begins. To repeat for the third time in this book, the value and importance of trial runs can never be overstated.

Extra Appraisals

The use of extra appraisals during the initial production can be very valuable. A start-up is characterized by the word "new." For this reason, a number of unusual circumstances which can cause the production of defective units often occurs during a start-up. One can never be certain that all contingencies of this type have been anticipated and prevented. Therefore, the employment of extra, nonroutine appraisal measures during the initial production can serve (a) to enhance the probability that an unanticipated quality defect will be rapidly detected before much finished product exhibiting the defect has been produced, (b) to give added assurance via increased sample sizes that completed production does adhere to quality standards, and (c) to enhance the probability of identifying segments of production which do not meet quality requirements. Relative to the latter point, on a hopefully seldom but as-needed basis, appraisal personnel should be available to cull failures from this kind of production so as to render it acceptable for the market. If the costs related to these added appraisals seem excessive or redundant, recall the discussion regarding the extreme importance of delivering the product in its intended form to each first-time user of the new product.

For better perspective, return briefly to the JEBB Company. During the first six months, 250 million bottles of soft drink were produced and sold. Assume that extra appraisals were used to cull out defects from the worst segments of production such that the overall crucial defect level was reduced from 0.50 percent to 0.25 percent. This action removed 625,000 crucial defects from the initial production. If every one of these deleted crucial defects had been sold to a first-time user who otherwise would have liked and repurchased the product, $195 million in profits would have been lost (assuming a 15-year life for the soft drink)! This is a worst-case scenario. However, certainly a significant number of these defects would have gone to the type of consumer described. It is very easy to justify temporary (one-time) appraisal costs for a contribution to profits of this magnitude.

CAUTION IS EXERCISED

The fifth trait of a profitable quality system is that *caution is exercised*. This is due to the fact that relatively small changes in the amount of money spent to employ P&A measures can cause very large changes in the total quality cost. Previously, this was referred to as the "leverage effect." It is depicted graphically in Figure 11-1. The curve represents a theoretical, generalized plot of the total quality cost (T) versus expenditures for preventive and appraisal measures (P&A). It is theoretical because it assumes that P&A measures are introduced in descending order of their ability to reduce T.

Refer to Figure 11-1. Starting at the far left, P&A expenditures are zero; consequently, failure costs (F) and T are equal and very high. Proceeding to the right, as P&A measures are introduced, the leverage ef-

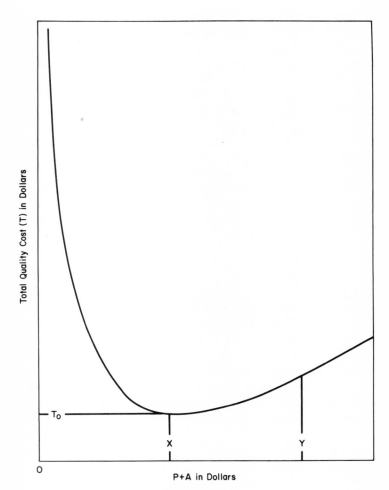

Scale: One unit of T = 2 units of P+A

FIGURE 11-1   The leverage effect.

fect is very much in evidence; large decreases in T result from relatively small P&A cash outlays. As X is approached, decreases in T continue, but they become smaller for a given P&A outlay, because the most attractive opportunities have already been exhausted. X represents the P&A expenditure at which the total quality cost is optimized, T_0. As we proceed from X to Y, additional P&A expenditures exceed the resulting failure cost reductions. Consequently, T increases by an amount less than the P&A cash outlay. Y represents the point at which all failures have been eliminated. No additional failure cost reductions are possible. Thus any further expenditures for P&A measures serve only to increase T by the exact amount of the expenditure.

It would be desirable to conduct all operations at the point X, to where all P&A measures which are economically justifiable have been incorporated into the quality system, and no inefficient P&A measures are present. In actuality, because of time limitations, this is rarely achievable by the time manufacturing operations commence. Operations to the left of X, T_0 involve the omission of valuable P&A actions. Due to the leverage effect, T can skyrocket completely out of control to a value very much higher than T_0. This was readily visible in Cases A and B. The amount by which T increases is unlimited. It is determined by the number of P&A measures omitted and the specific leverage effect associated with each one.

Operations to the right of X, T_0 involve the inclusion of all P&A measures which can decrease T economically plus all practical P&A measures which might decrease T economically but whose actual value is unknown. Increases in T above T_0 are restricted to the amount spent for P&A actions which later prove not to be economically justifiable. Case C clearly demonstrated that, until T can be optimized, it is much wiser and profitable to operate on the right side of X, T_0.

In order to be confident that this happens, caution must be exercised so that every potentially worthwhile, practical P&A measure is included in the quality system. Only when proof exists that one is not economically valuable should deletion occur. However, extreme care must be employed. Because of the leverage effect, the inopportune eradication of valuable P&A measure can permit T to increase out of control. This is precisely what did occur during Case C, year ten (C-10).

COMPETENT PERSONNEL

Management

A profitable quality system's sixth trait is the *presence of competent personnel.* During my almost two decades with the Procter & Gamble Company, I have had the pleasure of being associated with a multitude of highly competent quality system managers, including a significant number with exceptional ability. These capable individuals display common characteristics. First and foremost, each person thoroughly enjoys working as an integral part of a successful quality system, and each one brings a well-balanced blend of technical expertise, experience, common sense, and people skills to his or her particular job assignment. Each is highly skilled in the analytical process for identifying and solving problems. These individuals conduct themselves in a highly professional and ethical manner. Finally, these people exude a positive attitude reflecting determination that any reasonable objective can be achieved, and this contributes greatly to the fact that their objectives are indeed accomplished. It is this amalgam of strengths which enables a person to function as a competent manager in a profitable quality system.

Nonmanagement

The need for personnel competency within a quality system is not restricted to management. It is just as important that the nonmanagement employees who actually perform the work demonstrate proficiency. Personnel competency must pervade the entire quality system. This includes not only the personnel who are assigned directly to the quality function, but also personnel in the production function and in the production support functions, like maintenance. To varying degrees, all of these functions are a part of the total quality system.

In general, today's nonmanagement personnel are better educated and more informed than at any time in the past. To a large extent, this is due to the sophistication of the society in which we live and to the ready accessibility of "instant" communication facilities. Actually, the nonmanagement personnel of the 1980s possess many of the same abilities and skills as their managers. There are, however, two general exceptions to this similarity: Nonmanagement personnel have not received the same amount of formal management and/or technical education, and nonmanagement personnel possess a wealth of detailed "hands-on" knowledge about manufacturing operations. This knowledge, when it is considered and appropriately incorporated into the design of manufacturing systems, can be extremely useful for helping to prevent quality failure costs. (It can be equally useful in other areas not related to quality.) For example, in many chemical processes it is essential to monitor and control a number of parameters, such as temperatures, pressures, and flow rates, so that the resulting product will have the desired properties. Who should know better than the process operator where to best position the panel displaying the values of all of these parameters so that she or he can readily observe them while performing other related work? Therefore, because they possess many of the same abilities as managers and because they have in-depth knowledge of the details of manufacturing operations, nonmanagement employees of most businesses represent a vast potential resource for enhancing profits.

In an attempt to obtain the maximum benefit for quality systems from this enormous resource, a number of formal programs have been developed. The first of these surfaced in the early 1960s, and new ones are still being introduced. However, only a few have gained broad notoriety and use. These are briefly discussed below.

Zero Defects

The basic concept is that any job worth doing is worth doing right; this avoids the extra costs associated with having to do the job again or having to salvage or scrap the result. The specific objective of zero defects (ZD) programs is to instill throughout an entire organization a new attitude aimed at preventing failure costs. Many programs of this nature tailored to the needs of a particular company are reported in the literature under a variety of names. Examples include No Mistakes, PRIDE, Do It Right, Total Reliability, and Error Free Performance. These programs are characterized by a kickoff rally, employee pledge cards, posters, anniversary celebrations, formal awards ceremonies, and so on. A ZD program supplements an existing quality system; it is not a replacement for the system. Even among ZD program experts, a considerable difference of opinion exists as to whether such programs are motivational efforts capable only of generating short-term benefits or whether they can establish a permanent performance criterion reflecting perfection which results in the embellishment of profits over a long time interval.

Error Cause Removal

The basic concept is for management to tap worker knowledge regarding the identification of sources of failure costs. It is then management's responsibility to eliminate these trouble spots. An employee suggestion box is one form of an error cause removal (ECR) program. An ECR program can either be conducted separately or it can be included as a portion of a ZD program.

Quality Circles

The basic concept is for management to provide time for naturally occurring work groups (circles) to meet in order to attack and solve quality problems and/or to work on quality improvement projects. The groups are usually limited to a maximum of about ten people. After the circles have been organized, they are normally provided training on pertinent topics such as problem identification, analysis, and solving techniques or management techniques for priorizing projects. Actually, the circles concept is not limited to quality considerations. It can also be used to establish and maintain programs in other areas such as safety improvement or for cost reduction. The quality circles (QC) concept originated in Japan in the early 1960s and subsequently spread into the industries of the western world. In the United States, the popularity of QC programs has increased substantially starting in the late 1970s and extending into the 1980s. To illustrate, as of this writing the most recent issue of the American Society for Quality Control monthly magazine, *quality progress*, was forty-nine pages long. It contained eight different advertisements, ranging in size from one quarter page to an entire page, for seminars and/or consultation services regarding quality circles.

The literature contains numerous articles and several books reflecting successful applications of all three of these programs. However, almost all of them describe remedial situations. That is, the programs were initiated in order to rectify existing quality systems which were considered to be inadequate. The case studies demonstrated that waiting until this point in time to achieve an acceptable quality system can be a very expensive proposition.

GIVE THE EMPLOYEES THE OPPORTUNITY TO PARTICIPATE IN THE DESIGN OF THE QUALITY SYSTEM

Based on personal experience and on observing this aspect of management for a number of other projects, I am convinced that the key to utilizing the valuable worker resource to its maximum potential is to provide the opportunity for the employees to genuinely participate in the design of the quality system. Worker involvement should begin in the very early stages of quality system design and proceed for the project's life. This concept offers a number of advantages:

1. It enables maximum utilization of this vast resource during the very crucial time interval prior to start-up.

2. It goes a long way toward gaining the commitment of the quality system employees before start-up to operate the designed quality system such that the expected results are achieved.

3. It creates an environment in which the workers can realize that they do have a substantial amount of "say-so" in shaping their own industrial destiny.

4. It promotes an atmosphere of longer-term trust between management and employees.

One Prerequisite

The only prerequisite for introducing this concept is management's authentic belief in and commitment to its value. Actually, this concept is very similar to quality circles except that it requires initiation of the program at a specific point in time—when design of the quality system commences. One approach for employing this concept is to include a representative from each natural work group in each of the design activities which will significantly impact on the work group. These activities should include the major decision-making meetings. The representatives must be able to effectively communicate input resulting from the meetings of the workers (circles) to management. They must also be allowed to communicate candidly with management. Although employee involvement of this type can require a substantial investment of money and of management time, the benefits of significantly improved quality and productivity as manifested by profits will normally easily justify the investment.

SUMMARY

The six traits common to profitable quality systems include:

1. Top management understands the importance for and is committed to the control of product variability.

2. A comprehensive approach is used to develop and maintain the quality system.

3. The prevention of failures is a high priority.

4. An awareness of the extra importance of controlling a product's variability during its initial production stage is present.

5. Caution is exercised.

6. Competent personnel are employed.

Of these, traits **1** and **6** are the most important ones. It has been my observation that, for any portion of a business, competent people given top management commitment in the form of whatever resources are required can attain almost any reasonable goal. In the context of a quality system, the presence of competent quality personnel who are supported by top management make it very likely that traits **2**, **3**, **4**, and **5** will also be present. *The presence of all six traits makes it highly probable that the quality system will be highly profitable.*

PART FOUR
The Service Industries

In Parts I, II, and III, we discussed the management of profitable quality systems for profit-seeking businesses which market a manufactured product(s). Part IV will be devoted to a discussion of the same topic for profit-seeking businesses which market a benefit that is not a manufactured commodity. Businesses of this kind are usually included in a category labeled the "service industries," because the nonmanufactured benefit is in the form of a service to customers. Many businesses in the service industries market only a service. An airline markets transportation, a major league baseball team markets entertainment, a lawyer provides legal expertise, and a bank offers financial assistance. For many other businesses included in the service industries, the overall offering is a combination of a service and a manufactured product. For example, a restaurant markets both service in the form of convenience, atmosphere, and freedom from domestic chores, and a product in the form of its prepared food; the telephone company offers both telephones and telephone service.

For whatever portion of the overall offering of a business is a manufactured product, the considerations for managing a profitable quality system are identical to those covered in Parts I through III. To illustrate, in preparing food for its patrons, a successful restaurant will have considered all of the areas and most of the factors requiring effective management to control product variability as set forth in Part II. Product specifications will be established, like the acceptable temperature range of the food when it is served. Component specifications will be defined for all edible components, like "all beef will be choice grade." Suppliers for each edible component will have been appropriately qualified. For each offering on the menu a recipe will be available defining the relative proportion for each ingredient. Procedures for component and product handling will exist, like the length of time cauliflower can be stored before being cooked. Procedures will exist for preventing failure costs, like specification of the oven temperature and time to prepare medium-rare prime ribs of beef. Procedures will have been established as insurance against unexpected failure

161

costs, like a waiter checking back with guests after serving their dinner to determine if everything is satisfactory.

In this part of the book, we will deal exclusively with the considerations for developing and maintaining a profitable quality system for whatever portion of a business is a service. As you might expect, these considerations are not totally divorced from those for a manufactured commodity. To avoid redundancy, we shall only discuss in depth those factors which are unique or are substantially different than for manufactured products.

12 Quality System Management

The service industries constitute a large piece of the economy of the United States (and many other economically advanced nations). In general terms, the services which are offered by the businesses in this category provide (a) specialized expertise, such as that furnished by an attorney, a veterinarian, or an automotive repair garage; (b) a cost advantage, such as self-service gasoline; (c) a time savings, such as a fast-food restaurant; (d) a convenience, as offered by a resort hotel or a car rental agency; (e) a facility for satisfying a physical need, such as a bowling alley or a tennis club; or (f) a service for satisfying a mental need, such as a seminar or a symphony. The myriad of businesses which offer services of these types are quite diverse. In addition to those mentioned above, the service industries include forms of transportation (e.g., airlines), entertainment (e.g., professional football), utilities (e.g., electric power), financial assistance (e.g., stock broker), maintenance (e.g., plumber), medical assistance (e.g., hospitals), news media (e.g., radio), and retail stores (e.g., department stores).

To assist in understanding that the rather large number of retail outlets is a part of the nation's service economy, consider that most of these businesses do not manufacture the products they sell and that the same merchandise is often available through competitive businesses. In the extreme, identical products which were not manufactured by the retailer are offered for sale by competing businesses. This situation is closely approximated by the automobile dealerships for any particular make of car. In this circumstance, the retailer basically has two means of attracting customers who desire to purchase the specific make of car. This can be accomplished via a price advantage or via a quality of service advantage(s). The former topic is beyond the scope of this book. The service quality advantage can be present in many different ways. For example, it can be manifested in sales personnel who have earned trust, sales personnel who possess a deep knowledge of their salable products, a garage which performs maintenance accurately and within a reasonable time, or the proximity to a customer's residence or place of employment.

QUALITY DEFINED

In Part I, we defined "quality" as "the degree of excellence at an acceptable price and the control of variability at an acceptable cost." We then examined the three key parts of this definition in the context of a consumer or an industrial product. Let's now scrutinize this definition as it applies to a profit-seeking service.

Degree of Excellence

The degree of excellence is determined by the ability of the service when variability is being adequately controlled to deliver the intended benefit to customers and to manifest advantages relative to competition. For many years I have purchased one make of automobile from one particular dealership. A key reason for my loyalty to this business is the high degree of excellence which their maintenance department exhibits. Whenever my cars have required repair or preventive maintenance, this service department has delivered what was needed at an acceptable price. I can only recall one occasion when they were unable to find the source of a problem. Even in this case they informed me of their difficulty when I returned to pick up the car. They offered to do additional work whenever it was convenient for me to again leave the car. On that visit they were able to locate and solve the problem. Also, this service department demonstrates a number of distinct advantages relative to competition. For example, customers are treated courteously; because of its relatively large size, a broad bank of technical expertise and experience are available for dealing with problems; they take time to explain to customers what caused the malfunction and what actions had to be taken to correct it; and they usually get the job accomplished correctly in one visit.

One meaningful difference relative to manufactured products is that it may be difficult to obtain an accurate assessment of the degree of excellence of a service until just before, or even after, the start of business operations. Previously, for manufactured products, we discussed the critical importance of preventing quality problems before a business commences operations. For exactly the same reason, this is equally valid for the service industries. During the development of a new or improved product, a prototype normally becomes available at an early stage. This prototype (and replicas if needed) can be used to evaluate the product's degree of excellence. As soon as the prototype for a new type of popcorn popper has been constructed, it can be used to actually pop corn so as to determine how well the design is able to perform the intended function. Also, the advantages which the new popper possesses relative to competition can be ascertained by comparing the performance of units available in the marketplace with the performance of the prototype.

On the other hand, it may difficult to determine with confidence how well a particularly designed service is able to deliver the intended benefit in actual practice and when variability is adequately controlled until the real business facility can be used. Until that time, service simulations and knowledge or prior experience may have to be relied upon. However, in general, businesses will want to open relatively soon after their facility has been completed. This means that service businesses may have only a short time period available to address and complete the very important task of implementing changes so as to rectify degree of excellence deficiencies. For example, it would be difficult to determine with 100 percent certainty that the designed acoustical system for a new theatre was adequate until the theatre has been constructed, decorated, and furnished. By this time, the first scheduled performance in the theatre might only be weeks or days away. If at this point the acoustical system proves to be unsatisfactory, remedial actions will have to be swiftly enacted.

Control of Variability

The control of variability connotes that, to the extent permitted by the degree of excellence of a service, a very high number of business transactions (a) will deliver the intended benefit; (b) will be conducted in a safe manner and adhere to pertinent regulatory statutes; and (c) will not involve customer negatives which diminish the potential for future transactions.

As an illustration of (a), consider a fast-food franchise which has capably designed its service to provide the benefit of accommodating customer orders in 4 minutes or less. Suppose that over a given time frame this criterion was met for only 80 percent of orders placed because the personnel working behind the counter were conversing with each other rather than attending to their duties. This represents inadequate control of variability.

As an example of (b), suppose that in correcting a deficiency in a television set, the repair person leaves a loose electrical connection which can eventually lead to a short circuit. This also represents inadequate control of variability.

As an illustration of (c), I know of a person who contracted a particular real estate company and one of its salespersons to sell his house and to assist him in purchasing a new one with the desired features. It took the salesperson about 2 months to consummate both house sales. As a result, the client was satisfied, and the real estate agent was $3500 wealthier. Then the agent informed the client that $90 had been spent in out-of-pocket expenses to facilitate the sales. The agent asked to be reimbursed for that amount. The client obliged, but was extremely irritated to the point that he will never again do business with the agent or even with the company. The irritation stemmed not from the sum of the money, but rather because the agent spent the money without his consent. The agent would have been far wiser, since he had not consulted his client, to view the expenditure as a $90 investment which returned $3500. For the real estate company, this situation represents potential market failure costs relative to all future real estate dealings involving the client. This market failure occurred despite the fact that the intended benefit was delivered to the customer. It happened simply because of the manner in which the salesman conducted his business. Again, this is inadequate control of variability.

Money

Money is the third element of our quality definition. Just as for a manufactured commodity, a service must be marketed at an acceptable price to customers, and the control of variability must be accomplished at an acceptable cost to the business.

THE QUALITY COST CONCEPT

The utility of the quality cost concept as a powerful tool for assisting in managing profitable quality systems for manufactured commodities was comprehensively covered in Parts I and III. I am not personally familiar with any results from an application of this concept to a service business. Therefore, we shall only briefly and generally discuss the quality cost concept as a potential valuable tool for managing profitable quality systems for service businesses.

The discussion of the quality cost concept in Chapter 2 is sufficiently general to be applicable to any profit-seeking business. The only exception is the definition of the quality cost categories which were tailored to apply to a manufactured product. The main thrust of the discussion was to demonstrate that (a) an optimum total cost exists for operating the quality system of a business and (b) to conduct operations such that the actual total quality cost deviates meaningfully from optimum is to risk the loss of a substantial amount of profit which could be obtained.

Therefore, the quality costs for any business must be effectively managed.

Quality Costs

To ascertain whether the quality cost concept could be used in a service business, let's attempt to redefine the quality cost categories in the context of a service business.

Appraisal Costs

Appraisal costs would be expenses incurred to assess the quality of the service, of its components, or of operations. This would include the costs related to an inspector who evaluates the performance of an airlines' flight attendants; the cost of an auditor to review a car rental company's customer billings for accuracy; and the costs to inspect dry-cleaned garments for soil removal before customers reclaim them.

Internal Failure Costs

Internal failure costs might result when (a) potential or real inferior service is rectified before it is delivered to customers and (b) when the business is unable for a quality reason to perform its intended service. Examples of (a) would include the cost to a restaurant of discarding dishes which were chipped during washing; the cost to a bank for correcting errors detected prior to mailing their monthly statements to checking account users; and the costs for rerepairing a lawn mower when it is discovered prior to the owner calling for it that the original repair job was improperly performed. As an example of (b) consider a large automotive repair garage where one mechanic exclusively performs front-end alignments. Suppose the equipment used for this purpose breaks down because this particular mechanic misused it. The mechanic's idle time during this period constitutes an internal failure cost.

Market Failure Costs

Market failure costs might result from (a) inferior service being delivered to customers and (b) being unable to deliver the service when it is needed by the customer. Examples of (a) would include a monetary settlement to a restaurant patron who acquired a tongue laceration from a chipped drinking glass; customers who take their business elsewhere after receiving a $250 bill for automobile maintenance subsequent to obtaining an estimate of $75 for the job; and a patient who switches to a new dentist after repeatedly having to wait 1 to 2 hours beyond the scheduled appointment. As an example of (b), consider the front-end alignment equipment breakdown discussed above. Potential market failures occur if, owing to the malfunction, repairs are not completed when customers return to pick up their vehicles. Another example is when a car wash must close its doors in order to repair equipment. These circumstances provide customers with an opportunity to take their business elsewhere.

Preventive Costs

Preventive costs would be expenditures to eliminate or reduce appraisal costs and the occurrence of failure costs. This includes the development and implementation of procedures by airlines to minimize passenger dissatisfaction when an over-booked flight situation occurs; it includes the costs for educating a company's insurance agents in the specifics of a new kind of dental care insurance; and it includes the training of a plumbing company's personnel in the courtesies and amenities to be observed when on a customer's premises.

Similarity to Quality Costs for Manufactured Products

This discussion is very similar to the Part I discussion of quality cost categories pertaining to manufactured products. The utility of the quality cost concept for managing quality systems of manufactured products for profit has been demonstrated many times in actual practice and in Part III of this book. Part III also showed the vital importance of obtaining firm knowledge and control of the magnitude of market failure costs. For service businesses it may be even more critical to have this knowledge and control. This is because, in general, a service business encounters many more chances for market failures than a product. Think of a hotel guest who can experience a market failure in dealings with a bellhop, at the check-in desk, in the room, at the bar, in the coffee shop, on an elevator, in the parking lot, while checking out, and so on. Think also of the almost infinite number of circumstances which could generate a market failure for each of the above situations. An important attribute of the quality cost concept is that its use mandates that at least a reasonable grasp of market failure costs be available. Therefore, I conclude that the quality cost concept might also be a powerful tool for helping to manage quality systems and, hence, embellishing profits for the service industries.

AREAS OF MANAGEMENT RESPONSIBILITY

This section will cover the areas of responsibility which must be effectively managed in order to adequately control the quality variability of a service. These basic areas are very similar to those covered in Part II for a manufactured item. However, some of the factors which need to be considered to manage the respective areas in the service industries must be viewed from an entirely different perspective. Attention will be focused on these factors during the following discussion.

Service Specifications

The first area of responsibility which must be addressed is the *establishment of all of the service specifications* which define the limits of acceptable quality for a service. An example of one service specifcation for a real estate company might be that "a request to see any listed piece of property will be honored within 24 hours." Some, perhaps a great many, service businesses do not organize all of their pertinent specifications into a formal document analogous to the Finished Product Specification commonly employed for a manufactured commodity. Instead, these specifications may be included as a part of operating procedures, or they may even be communicated orally. In order to ensure that all of the specifications for a business are clearly understood and readily accessible to all employees, I strongly favor the accumulation of these specifications into an overall Service Specification, or its equivalent.

Attributes

It can be substantially more difficult for a service as opposed to a manufactured commodity to identify the attributes which are of sufficient importance to warrant a specification. This is because of the existence of a fundamental difference in the way in which a customer judges the quality of a service versus that of a product. For a product, this judgment is usually based solely on *what* is purchased. For a service, however, the quality evaluation often depends not only on what the customer buys, but also on *how* the benefit is delivered.

To illustrate, consider a man who buys an electric clock. The man will probably be satisfied with the manufacturer's quality after he determines that what he purchased, the clock, tells time accurately, performs safely, and possesses no aesthetically displeasing flaws. Now suppose that after several years, he takes the clock to a maintenance shop for a needed repair. When he returns to collect the clock, he experiences a 20-minute delay while the needs of other customers are being accommodated. For this situation, the man may be discontented with the quality of the repair service even after he determines that what he purchased, clock maintenance, was quite satisfactory. The clock again tells time accurately, performs safely, and possesses no aesthetic deficiencies. However, how it was received (with personal inconvenience) might meaningfully influence his overall assessment of the quality of the service. As a further example, have you ever heard someone remark that a particular physician knows his medicine well, but that his "bedside manner" leaves much to be desired?

Because of its highly subjective nature, the identification of the key customer attributes associated with the "how element" of a service can be a difficult task. That is, different people can react in completely different ways to the manner in which a particular service is rendered. An insurance agent who relates an ethnically oriented joke during the course of conducting business with potential clients might find that a person of the same ethnic background reacts quite negatively, whereas a person of another culture might react neutrally, or even favorably. Furthermore, a given person may react quite differently at different points in time to the same service. Following a very difficult and tiring day at the office, a woman may become highly vexed when she discovers on the way home that the dry cleaner with the suit she intended to wear the next day has already closed for the evening. The same woman might find the same situation tolerable subsequent to a pleasant day at work when she accomplished several important objectives.

In net, how a service is delivered can profoundly influence a customer's decision to reuse the service and to purchase additional services offered by the business. Therefore, a service business must know what the key customer attributes are for the "how element" of its service.

Limits

The limits which are established for each vital attribute of a service should include only service that is known to be acceptable to customers. The reason for this is identical to the reason discussed for the same factor in Part II for manufactured products. I read in the newspaper that a broadcaster for a radio station had been relieved of his responsibilities because of a weak voice. While answering questions about the matter, an executive at the station was reported as saying words to the effect that he didn't know whether listeners objected to the announcer's voice, but that management did. The implication was that management had developed limits regarding the voice quality of broadcasters that they knew were acceptable to their listeners, and that the voice of this specific announcer fell beyond those limits into an area where acceptability was unknown. Management had only two reasonable alternatives: determine the acceptability of his voice to listeners or obtain a person with a voice known to be in the satisfactory range. Had the former option been selected, the latter would also have had to be pursued if it had turned out that a significant number of listeners did indeed object to his voice characteristics.

The Effect of Outstanding Employees

A feature which is peculiar to the service industries is the potential effect of an individual employee(s) who has intrinsically established service specifications that are substantially more stringent than those set by the business. When this occurs, the profits of a business can be handsomely embellished, because the quality of service which that individual(s) provides can actually become the motivation for customers to purchase the service from that particular firm. The beneficial effect of an employee(s) of this kind is more readily evident for smaller businesses.

One day shortly after I moved to Cincinnati, I wanted to buy a nice piece of jewelry as a present. When I entered a particular, well-respected, local jewelry store, there were perhaps five salespeople and one other customer present. The sales personnel appeared to be busy chatting among themselves or making alterations to their display cases. After browsing through the store for a few minutes without seeing any item which was particularly suitable for my need and without being approached by a salesperson, I was about to exit when a young sales lady entered through a side door and immediatly inquired if she could be of assistance. This woman was pleasant and very knowledgeable about the store's merchandise. The result was that I bought a moderately expensive piece of jewelry. Subsequently, I purchased all my jewelry needs through this woman. Over the years, not only did she become familiar with my personal likes and dislikes in jewelry products, but, probably via comments that I made, she acquired a "feel" for the personal tastes of the people for whom I bought the jewelry. Whenever I entered the store, I was always greeted with a cheery "hello," and if she happened to be busy with another customer, which was usually the situation, she would add, "I'll be with you just as soon as I finish with _____." I always waited. Very seldom was I ever approached by another salesperson either when I entered the store or while I was waiting. Certainly the relatively few, moderately priced purchases which I made over these years contributed only a drop in the bucket to this firm's profit statement. However, judging from the facts that, whenever I entered the store, this specific salesperson was virtually always occupied with another customer; that she appeared to offer all of her customers the same courtesy, respect, and jewelry expertise as she did me; and that the other sales personnel appeared to demonstrate very little initiative toward customers, it would not be at all surprising for me to learn that her quality of service did contribute a very measurable amount to the profits of this company. A few years ago I stopped into the store one day about noon. Since my favorite saleslady was not present, I asked another salesperson when she was expected back from lunch. I was informed that she had moved her residence to a distant city. The salesperson offered no additional assistance. Although I have returned to this store a few times since, I have not bought any more jewelry there.

Exceptional quality owing to the very high quality standards of individuals is more apt to positively and meaningfully affect the profits of a service business than of one which markets a manufactured product. The primary reason is that for a goodly number of services the complete customer transaction is handled by a single employee. The above example typifies this. On the other hand, in today's world of mass production techniques, the extraordinary quality efforts of a few individuals can be diluted by the remaining people and automated equipment involved in a manufacturing process.

Overall Design of the Service

Finally, the overall design of any service must provide the ability for all service specifications to be met. Suppose a car rental company has a specification pertaining to their airport locations that "all customers will receive the keys to their rented car within 5 minutes after they come to the counter." To ensure that this specification can be adhered to, the car rental company must staff the desk with a sufficient number of employees at any given time to accommodate the expected number of customers at that time.

Components

A second area of responsibility which must be effectively addressed is all of the considerations for dealing with components. It is not easy to define the word "component" so that it applies to all of the highly diverse types of businesses which comprise the service industries. The definition which I believe is most applicable is: *A component is anything which customers view as being a part of the service or as directly assisting in the delivery of the service.* In the context of this definition there are five basic kinds of components.

1. Items Which Become Part of a Manufactured Product

Items which become a part of a manufactured product marketed by a service business as a portion of its total offering. An example is the ingredients to produce the food in a restaurant. The considerations for managing components of this type are identical to those discussed in Part II for components of manufactured products.

2. Items Seen or Used by Patrons

Items that are seen and/or used by patrons in the same form as they are received by the business. Examples include soap in hotel rooms, printed material distributed at seminars, or pamphlets handed out by banks describing the details of their checking account service. Since these components go straight through the business without changing, it is important to incorporate adequate preventive and appraisal measures so as to minimize the risk of potential market failures. To illustrate, imagine your reaction to unwrapping a hotel room bar of soap to find a dead water bug on the soap surface.

3. Recycled Items

Items which are recycled within the business facility. This would include the silverware and dishes used in a restaurant. The considerations are again similar to those covered in Part II regarding components for manufactured products. In addition, attention must be given to the manner in which these components are prepared for reuse and maintained in that condition from the end of one cycle to the beginning of another.

4. Equipment

Equipment used to assist in imparting the service. This might include the cash register in a department store, a bank's computer for handling after normal hours banking needs, or automatic pin-setting equipment in a bowling alley. The important quality factors for this type of component are the purchase of reliable equipment, obtaining assurance that replacement parts will be speedily available when needed, adopting a sound preventive maintenance program so as to minimize breakdowns during operating hours, and having an established back-up plan so that customers will not become disgruntled should a breakdown actually occur.

I was in a relatively large branch of a large grocery store chain when the computer used to verify the satisfactory check-cashing status for regular patrons experienced a malfunction. While I was in the check-out line, the woman immediately in front of me, who I happened to know, desired to pay her $18.11 purchase via a check. She displayed her validated computer card to the cashier and volunteered to show other identification. After inspecting the check, the cashier announced in a disrespectful and sufficiently loud voice so that all people in close proximity could readily hear that she would not accept a check drawn from an out-of-town bank under any circumstances. Her tone implied that the check was probably bad anyway. The customer tried to explain that she had shopped there for years and had always used the same checking account. After giving the customer further verbal abuse, the cashier finally agreed to speak with the store manager, who approved the check. The customer was highly provoked and embarrassed by the entire episode which would probably never have happened had the computer not broken down. Even so, it probably would have been avoided if the store had a previously developed back-up plan to cover this situation. Eight months later the woman informed me that subsequently she had not returned to any of the store's branches. This real market failure occurred over an $18.11 sale. This woman shops for her family of five. How much money do you think she spends annually for items sold in grocery stores?

5. *Personnel*

Clearly, the most important component of a service is *personnel*. The face-to-face contact between employees and customers is a major characteristic of service businesses. Thus, the quality of these contacts can have an immense impact on the profits of a service business. In addition, my definition of "component" can apply to some employees who do not normally experience direct customer contact. Consider airline passengers who experience damage to their luggage or its contents. In all likelihood these passengers will view the personnel involved in transferring suitcases from their point of embarkation to their destination as directly assisting in the delivery of the service.

To adequately control the variability of components which are included in items 1 through 4 requires the competent management of the same basic factors set forth for manufactured products in Part II under "Components" and "Manufacturing Operations." It is true that for service industry components of this kind, many of the relevant factors will deserve different emphasis and treatment than for products, but each one should be considered for appropriate action.

Employees as Components

Considering some employees of a business as integral components of a marketed offering is unique to the service industries. The most crucial factor to be managed to maximize the probability of transferring acceptable quality service via people to customers is the utilization of capable people in these jobs. A prerequisite for attempting to accomplish this noble objective is that the managers who have authority to hire new employees and to select personnel for specific job assignments be excellent judges of a person's mettle and abilities. More specifically, these managers must possess outstanding acumen for evaluating one's (a) general incentive to excel, (b) ability to handle particular jobs, and (c) integrity. To accomplish (b), these managers must know the specific skills needed to perform each pertinent job. Although the above formula is right on target for achieving the stated goal, it should come as no surprise to anyone that managers who actually possess the needed acumen are scarce, and even the very best perform with an accuracy below 100 percent.

In 1981, one of the best-known and most respected newspapers in the United States suffered extreme embarrassment and at least a significant dent in its fine reputation for quality reporting. One of this particular newspaper's main assets is its ability to identify, attract, and retain quality reporters. Yet this appears to have been the basic cause of the problem. A talented, young person reported a story which received national recognition. Later, it was determined that the fundamental theme and the main character in the story were fabrications. Subsequent checks revealed that some key items in this reporter's application to the newspaper for employment were also false. The inference is that the managers responsible for identifying and attracting new talent for this newspaper, and who had a proven record of success, were apparently sufficiently impressed by this reporter so as to deem it unnecessary to verify the contents of the employment application. Even for expertly trained managers with exceptional innate ability for such, it is very difficult to thoroughly judge a person's character and abilities in a short time period. However, because of the vital importance of doing it, particularly in the service industries, we must strive to the best of our abilities to achieve this objective.

Operating Procedures to Prevent Failure Costs

Another area requiring sound management is the *development and implementation of operating procedures to prevent potential quality failures.* The utilization of preventive measures for avoiding or reducing failures for service businesses is very similar and every bit as important as the use of these measures for manufactured products. However, the service businesses are so varied in nature that it is virtually impossible to categorize preventive measures as we did for products. For example, there are very few similarities between the way in which a professional football team provides entertainment and the way in which a plumber repairs a leaking faucet. Consequently, many of the factors which must be considered for preventive measures are quite different for these occupations. Therefore, the primary approach for incorporating prevention is to anticipate to the greatest practical extent for a given service business the potential quality failures that might occur. Then effective and pragmatic measures should be instituted to preclude the occurrence of these situations, or at least to minimize their effect should they occur.

The Value of Dress Rehearsals

One outstanding means for anticipating failures is the utilization of dress rehearsals as early as practical prior to the opening of a service business, or before implementing changes to the service. Everything discussed in Part III concerning the importance and value of trial runs for a product applies equally to dress rehearsals for a service. They provide the capability for uncovering *un*anticipated real and potential failures so that these become anticipated and can be prevented prior to start-up. Dress rehearsals also serve to resolve doubts and unanswered questions. To illustrate, after a new grocery store has been constructed and stocked with merchandise, and before it opens for business, store management might congregate a number of people in order to simulate store operations. They might want to see if the allotted space is sufficient to accommodate a given number of customers. They might also wish to compare the average actual time required for these "customers" to locate and obtain a list of specific grocery items versus the expected time to complete the list. Other kinds of dress rehearsals for service businesses include practice sessions for an orchestra in preparation for a performance, pro baseball's springtime Grapefruit League, and role playing by stock brokers, bankers, and real estate agents simulating potential situations which might be encountered during normal business operations.

The Value of Employee Experience

Another tool for anticipating quality failures is through the experience of employed personnel. To illustrate, assume that a new dry cleaner is about to open for business. The plan is for one employee to unlock the building each morning at 7:00 AM and to handle the patrons at the counter. A manager with previous experience in this type of business will certainly realize that sooner or later this employee will be absent because of illness. The result will be that the business will not open at the scheduled time. Consequently, customers may depart annoyed that they could not leave their soiled garments early in the morning for fast service. The experienced manager will have anticipated this eventuality and will have formulated a back-up plan. Then, when the telephone call does arrive at 6:30 AM some morning indicating that the employee is sick, the back-up plan can rapidly be placed into effect. Time will not be consumed deciding on a course of action and attempting to make it happen. The business can begin its daily operation as usual, thereby preventing potential market failures.

Identify Potential Problems Before They Become Real Ones

The key to an effective program for preventing inferior quality in any business is the identification of possible trouble spots before they yield real problems. Especially for service business, where direct contact between employees and customers frequently occurs, management should continually examine its operations for "snakes waiting to bite." The following example demonstrates how at times this can be so simple to do that it can be overlooked. For her ninth birthday my daughter wanted to invite eleven friends to a bowling party. Two weeks in advance we reserved three lanes at a nearby, large bowling facility for 2:00 PM on the appropriate Saturday afternoon. As we, twelve children and two adults, arrived at the lanes at the designated time, we noted that the parking lot appeared to be abnormally full. When we identified ourselves to the proprietor, he immediately began to explain the situation. Subsequent to accepting our reservation, it seems that a business firm offered to rent the entire facility for an afternoon outing. The owner said that he was unable to inform us of the difficulty because the person who took our reservation had only recorded the date, time, and that three lanes would be needed. Apparently neither our name nor telephone number had been noted. This was prevention error number 1. For several minutes I attempted to persuade the owner to empathize with the frustrations of the twelve youngsters. Still, he offered no "further" assistance. Then we noticed that exactly three alleys at the far end of the facility were not being used. We obtained permission from the ranking member of the business outing for the kids to use these lanes. However, the proprietor adamantly refused to allow us to use even those three vacant alleys on the basis that the children might interfere with the adults on the adjoining alley. At this point, I offered the proprietor my descriptive opinion of his ability to operate his business. Just as we were about to depart for a close-by ice cream parlor, the owner approached me to say that if we desired he could telephone a smaller bowling establishment located about a mile away to see if they had three alleys immediately available. We quickly agreed, and the children enjoyed a pleasant afternoon of bowling. The next time we host an outing of this type, we'll go directly to this smaller facility.

Now let's critique this incident. Had the owner paused to seriously evaluate the situation when it developed, he certainly could have anticipated that disappointment, frustration, and animosity would result when the birthday party arrived at his lanes. Realizing this he could have taken appropriate preventive measures. For example, he could have prevented, or at least drastically reduced, the ill will which resulted by simply placing the same telephone call to the same other bowling facility before we arrived. Then, after explaining the situation to us, he could have immediately offered a viable alternative which would have relieved our major anxieties of not disappointing the children and of not causing embarrassment to our daughter. We would have been only mildly inconvenienced. For this particular scenario the cost would have been negligible for preventing the ill will afforded us and the owner's loss of 15 minutes in dealing with me instead of serving his primary interest, the larger bowling party. Just as with manufactured commodities, the cost of preventive measures is usually small relative to the benefit(s) received.

Procedures to Restrain Potentially Disastrous Failure Costs

For a few kinds of potential service quality failures, even when they are anticipated, it may not be possible or practical to prevent their occurrence with 100 percent certainty. If the consequences of such an occurrence could be catastrophic, it is prudent to consider the adoption of additional preventive measures which have the capability for restraining failure costs from ballooning totally out of control should the event actually take place. Examples of this would include a physician's insurance against malpractice suits and an airline's insurance in the event of a crash.

Personnel Training

One factor which must be considered comprehensively and in depth for an appropriate prevention program in any service business is the need for personnel training. As an example of the benefits which are derivable from effective employee training, return to the jewelry store scenario cited previously. Think of the additional sales and, hence, profits which might be available to this enterprise if their sales personnel were merely refreshed in the art of assisting patrons in satisfying their jewelry needs. The cost of a preventive (training) program to accomplish this goal should be small.

Initiate Action to Avoid the Recurrence of Significant Failure Costs

Despite technically sound and comprehensive preventive programs, quality failures can still occur in service businesses, just as in businesses which manufacture products. Quality failures occur because the event was not anticipated or because the preventive measures being employed were not adequate or were not being properly carried out. Regardless of the reason, when quality failures happen, action must be swiftly and efficiently taken to avoid a recurrence.

A local auditorium began marketing live theatrical performances which consisted mainly of the traveling companies of Broadway hits. Capital for the enterprise was raised by a campaign, which sold a significant number of season subscriptions. Tickets were relatively expensive. Because this particular auditorium did not have a really good acoustical system, each show supplied its own supplemental sound equipment. As a result, the clarity and loudness of on-stage verbal exchanges left much to be desired. In fact, the sound was so poor for some plays that a number of the audience left at the intermission. Many people were grumbling that because they were not obtaining real value for their money, they would not renew their season tickets for the following year. Realizing the deteriorating situation, the auditorium decided to install an acceptable and permanent acoustics system for the auditorium prior to the start of ticket sales for the next year. Immediately, a letter was addressed to all season ticket holders apologizing for the acoustics problems, informing them of the plans to install a new system, and requesting their continued patronage. This is an example of swift action to remedy potential service quality market failures. Time will be the judge of how efficient this remedial action will be.

In net, a sound preventive program is a necessity for ensuring service quality. Planning ahead is a prerequisite for achieving this objective.

Appraisals

Another area of responsibility within the service industries which must be well managed is *appraisals.* In Part II, we dicussed the utility of conducting appraisals at the manufacturing site to ensure the quality of finished product before being shipped into the trade. For a number of service businesses, a similar opportunity exists to assess service before it is delivered to the customer. A repair service for small electrical appliances can actually operate a radio, an electric frying pan, or a toaster to be certain that it functions properly before the owner arrives to retrieve the item. If this opportunity is available, its merits should be fully considered.

In the extreme, when it is possible and economically practical to appraise 100 percent of service work before it is returned, this circumstance by itself can contribute to one's motivation to purchase the service from that business. Earlier I mentioned that a key reason for my loyalty to a specific auto dealership is their outstanding maintenance department. One aspect of their service, which contributes largely to their superiority, is that cars are road tested after they are repaired. If the company is not satisfied with the result, additional maintenance is performed. Thus, I don't have to worry that while driving the car home I will discover that the troublesome item was not repaired sufficiently. In other words, a factor which contributes importantly to my incentive for dealing exclusively with this company is that they appraise their work before it reaches the customer.

On the other hand, a large number of service businesses offer their benefit in a manner that does not yield a chance for appraisal between the time it is performed and the time it is received by customers. This circumstance almost always exists during direct transactions between a business and its patrons. There is no chance to appraise the quality of remarks made by a hotel check-out clerk before these comments are received by customers paying their bills. There is no opportunity to evaluate the quality of service rendered by a restaurant waiter in serving culinary selections to guests until after these customers have received their meals. Circumstances of this kind may represent a minute portion of the overall service rendered, but we all know that they can have an enormous impact upon the quality image which customers retain of the business. In other words, because for situations of this type there is no opportunity via appraisal to restrict inferior service quality to an internal failure, any substandard service automatically becomes a potential market failure.

The effect of a significant number of market failures to a service business, just as for a business which manufactures a product, is to substantially decrease profits. In the extreme, this can be just as fatal for a service as for a product. Therefore, any business which offers a service, especially when the service does not permit a quality appraisal opportunity before being received by the customer, should seriously consider the value of conducting post-service appraisals. This is precisely the reason that we are requested to fill out critique sheets following airplane travel, attendance at seminars, and so on. Other alternatives for conducting appraisals of this nature are by telephone or by mail. Regardless of the means employed, the primary objective of these appraisals is to obtain and maintain a firm grasp on the customer's opinion of the quality of the service being marketed. Without this knowledge it is impossible to manage the contribution of service quality to the profits of a company.

The quality of service being marketed by a business should be continuously appraised. This is especially important to a small service business in which one person can dramatically influence the overall quality level. Consider a neighborhood drug store operated by the owner, who we shall call Ms. Smith, and two employees, a daytime and an evening clerk. Suppose that the store's clientele generally regard the overall service quality as entirely satisfactory. Then the evening clerk begins to experience marital problems and becomes grumpy, unfriendly, and easily irritable. Suppose that because Ms. Smith has limited contact with the evening clerk, she does not immediately detect the personality change. Unless Ms. Smith remains closely attuned to her customer's evaluation of the drug store's quality of service, she may very well find without knowing the reason why that sales and profits have substantially diminished.

Quality System Audits

Finally, the value of quality audits should be fully considered by service businesses. Quality's contribution to profits is predicated upon the preventive and appraisal measures which have been introduced to respectively avoid quality failures and assure service quality. The primary objective of an audit is to provide assurance that these measures are operating and that they are being performed as intended. An example is a person who travels around the country comparing the actual versus the expected quality performance for the various restaurants affiliated with a hotel chain. The key elements of a quality audit for a service are virtually identical to those discussed for a product in Part II.

SUMMARY

The areas of responsibility and the respective factors which must be effectively managed in order for the quality systems of service businesses to contribute substantially to the profits of those firms are basically the same as for manufactured commodities. It is only the emphasis on specific areas and factors that differs significantly.

13 Quality System Traits

Previously, we dicussed the traits which when managed into a manufactured product's quality system greatly improve the chances of that system for furnishing substantial profits to the company. In this chapter, we shall examine the applicability of these traits to the quality systems of businesses included in the service industries.

TOP MANAGEMENT COMMITMENT

The first trait is the *commitment of top management* to control the quality of its marketable offering to a level acceptable to customers. The presence of this trait is a prerequisite to the development and maintenance of a profitable quality system in the service industries. The reasons are identical to those discussed for manufactured products. In addition, because of the direct contact which naturally occurs between most service businesses and their patrons, the absence of this trait from a quality system is frequently more readily discernible to service users than to buyers of a product. When this deficiency is detected, it is almost always highly objectionable to customers.

A regional chain of discount department stores operated a rather large branch near my home. Occasionally, I visited the store to satisfy a random need. Almost always, the merchandise was disorganized and sloppily arranged, the employees were unable or unwilling to give assistance, and the store was generally unclean. Even when the branch manager was present in the retail sales area, nothing appeared to change. Subsequently, I learned that this specific branch was quite typical of all of the company's retail outlets. Evidently, the discount chain's general management did not regard the providing of quality service to patrons as being of prime importance. Not surprisingly, the conditions at least at the store in my locale progressively deteriorated. Then the company declared bankruptcy. The particular branch store was purchased by another company which operated a chain of discount department stores. Almost instantaneously, the store was cleaned up and rendered more attractive; the merchandise was organized, neatly arranged, and continuously maintained that way; and the employees became available for customer assistance. I have seen the new store manager speak directly, but discreetly and courteously, to employees when he discovered a situation in the store that he desired to alter. This store has now conducted operations for a number of years. From all apparent indications it is quite prosperous. Other branches of this chain which I have been in present a similar image. Apparently, the management of this company is keenly aware of the profit value of an outstanding quality system and is, therefore, committed to its achievement.

One indicator that often signals the absence of top management support for quality and which, when it occurs, is frequently noticeable to users of a service is the lack of sufficient resources for the service to be performed satisfactorily. Without management backing for quality, it is frequently very difficult for working-level employees to obtain the resources which they need in order to deliver service quality. To illustrate, recall the episode in the very first chapter of this book pertaining to the acquisition of stereo units for my sons. In brief, as the result of experiencing a 50 percent level for a particular brand and model, I expressed reluctance to purchase any additional products manufactured by this company. Later, unfortunately, my lack of confidence in this company's ability or desire to control quality proved to be well founded.

The following scenario took place about 5 months after purchase of the stereos. The units were covered by a 3-month warranty. While listening to a record, one of my sons detected the type of malodor associated with an electrical fire. Fortunately, this 13-year-old was astute enough to immediately disengage the electrical plug from the wall outlet. By doing so he may well have prevented a major problem. The instruction manual which accompanied the stereo directed customers to obtain information regarding authorized service dealers by dialing a specific toll-free telephone number. Upon doing so, I was given the names of three "authorized" service dealers in my general vicinity. I contacted each one by telephone. The first stated that they no longer serviced this brand because they could not obtain replacement parts from the manufacturer. The second "authorized" service center had gone out of business. The third said that they no longer serviced this brand, offering no explanation. I re-called the toll-free number and informed the company of my dilemma. They supplied me with the names of three additional "authorized" dealers. It turned out that the first no longer serviced the brand because they were unable to obtain electrical schematic diagrams from the marketer. The second and third ones no longer serviced the brand because they couldn't obtain replacement parts from the producer. At this point I was thoroughly disgusted.

I re-called the toll-free number and asked to speak to the supervisor, whom I shall call Ms. Jones. After I related the entire episode to her, she spent 3 minutes explaining to me that the unit was no longer covered by warranty. Finally I was able to inform her that I was perfectly agreeable to paying for the necessary repairs and that all I desired from her company was the name of an authentic authorized service dealer. She promised to call me back with this information. Two days later neither my office nor my home had received a call from this company. I called again only to find that Ms. Jones was on vacation and would return in 2 weeks. I asked to speak with her supervisor, whom I shall call Mr. Brown. I was told that he was busy and would have to return my call. He never did. This situation was repeated three times. I have no evidence that Mr. Brown ever attempted to contact me. However, during my last call to this company I happened to speak with a pleasant young lady who said she would get me the desired information. Several hours later she called with the name of a newly opened service center. Within a week, the damage to the stereo created by the electrical fire had been repaired.

To state it mildly, my son and I were totally frustrated and angered by this entire incident. After regaining my composure relative to the marketer of the stereo, I reasoned that its upper management might be concerned about and appreciate being made aware of the service quality which I received. Consequently, I wrote a brief and factual letter to its president relating the episode. I distributed copies to Ms. Jones and Mr. Brown, and I especially mentioned the name of the lady who had finally filled my request. As of this writing, more than 6 months have elapsed. I have yet to receive a reply of any kind. In retrospect, it would not be surprising to learn that the difficulty which the "authorized" service centers experienced in obtaining repair parts could be directly traced to the lack of top management commitment to provide service quality. When upper management views a subject as unimportant, there is little incentive for middle and lower management to do otherwise. It will be interesting to me to observe the profit and loss statement for this company over the next several years.

THE QUALITY SYSTEM IS COMPREHENSIVE, EMPHASIZES PREVENTION, PLACES EXTRA EMPHASIS ON QUALITY DURING THE OPENING OF A BUSINESS, AND EXERCISES CAUTION

Traits two through five of successful quality systems are, respectively: *the system comprehensively covers all aspects of quality; heavy emphasis is given to the prevention of failures; personnel are attuned to the extra importance of control-*

ling variability during the initial marketing phase of the service; and *caution is excerised.* Any further discussion of the need for and utility of these four characteristics in the quality system for a service would closely parallel the discourse for the same traits as they pertain to the quality system of a manufactured product. In order to avoid repetition, the reader is referred to the coverage of these topics in Chapter 11 in the context of consumer and industrial commodities.

COMPETENT PERSONNEL

The sixth trait, and certainly one of the most important, is *the employment of competent personnel to manage and to operate the quality system*. As essential as this trait is in the management and operation of a quality system for a manufactured item, its presence is even more vital to the quality system for a service. The reason for the added importance is again owing to the fact that a general characteristic of a service business is that at least a fraction of its operating personnel deal directly with the general public.

One day after work I stopped at a small, convenience-item grocery store to buy some milk which was needed at home. After obtaining the milk from the refrigerated shelf, I proceeded to the cash register. Three customers were in line ahead of me. The only employee visible in the entire store was a nice-looking young man who was handling the checkout line. Two of the customers in front of me asked the employee an inordinate number of questions about their purchases. More than 5 minutes elapsed while I waited to pay. During the interim, I was considering alternate convenience stores where I might in the future transact small purchases of this type without experiencing such a delay. When it finally became my turn to check out, the young man appreciatively thanked me for waiting so long. This single action defused much of my frustration, and subsequently I have made many purchases at this store. The prevention of this market failure resulted solely from the competence of this employee in not only recognizing the emergence of a service quality problem, but in taking the initiative to implement an immediate action which did in fact alleviate it. Employee competence is probably the best ingredient in the quality system of a service business for dealing with the myriad of potentially negative situations that can present themselves. This is because most of these situations require immediate attention and action, and many of them involve peculiar circumstances.

Ability to Attract New Business

Lets's now consider a different facet of this trait. The presence of competent personnel in the quality system of a service business can by itself be directly responsible for attracting new business and thereby generating additional profits. I happen to know a real estate salesperson for a company in a city where I used to reside who is a perfect example of this phenomenon. He was kind enough to share with me a number of letters which he received subsequent to the completion of real estate transactions. Following are excerpts from a few of these letters:

Letter No. 1   "I feel that you have gone above and beyond the usual in taking care of me. Thanks. Also, when we buy another piece of property, rest assured that we will be dealing with you."

Letter No. 2   "We are delighted that our house has been sold. Equally gratifying was the courtesy, honesty, and patience shown us. We value your friendship and will not hesitate to recommend you to friends."

Letter No. 3   "I appreciate the help you gave me in purchasing and selling my home. I admire you very much. You are a fine fellow and an all-around good salesperson. I have great confidence in your honesty and in the efficient manner in which you develop a business transaction."

Letter No. 4   (From the executor of a will) "I have the brochures on the _____ property and they are magnificent! You are to be congratulated on a truly ultraprofessional job. The brochures should produce a fast sale of the property."

I could continue, however, it is evident from these letters that this gentleman's competence in consummating real estate transactions with efficiency, respect for people, and integrity is readily visible to many of his clients, and it actually serves as the foundation for potential future business. Another example showing the same type of ability was related in the previous chapter about the competence of a saleslady in a jewelry store. Quality system personnel who demonstrate a competence level of this magnitude are the exception rather than the rule. However, their worth relative to the profits of a business is obvious.

Ability to Lose Business

On the other hand, delinquency in incorporating the traits of competent personnel into the quality system for a service can lead to the inadequate control of variability for the service and ultimately to quality market failures. Some years ago when I moved to Cincinnati, I placed my automobile and homeowner insurance with a particular insurance agency and agent for what I considered to be valid reasons at that time. A number of years later I experienced the only car accident I have ever had. While backing up in a parking lot, I slightly dented the rear fender of another car. The repair work was estimated at $145. Upon contacting the insurance agent, he asked that I stop by his office. After I arrived, he briefly explained that since my insurance coverage involved a $100 deductible clause, I could only collect $45 maximum from the company. He recommended against doing so, because the premium for my coverage would be increased. Then he suggested that instead of concerning ourselves with this "minor problem," we discuss the advantages of applying his financial expertise to managing my investment portfolio. He may have been correct regarding the collection of the $45 from the insurance company. However, I was quite distressed after faithfully paying the premium for a number of years not to be compensated for this small incident; I was perturbed at his lack of concern for not providing me with any service; and I was appalled by his poor judgment, since my investment portfolio was too small to merit any degree of management sophistication. At the earliest practical time, my insurance needs were transferred to another company and agent.

In a sentence, the quality system of a service business must be comprised of competent personnel in order to have even a reasonable chance of contributing anything near its full profit potential to the business.

QUALITY SYSTEM MANAGEMENT IS FUNDAMENTALLY THE SAME FOR SERVICES AND PRODUCTS

The discussion contained in Part IV pertaining to the development and maintenance of profitable quality systems for service businesses is very similar to the treatment of the same subject contained in Parts I, II, and III for businesses that manufacture a product. This is a key point. *The traits which must be managed into a quality system and the areas of responsibility which that system must effectively manage are basically the same regardless of whether the marketed offering is a product or a service.* In general, for a service there will be less emphasis on the management of things and more on the management of people. Also, many of the factors which must be considered in order to manage the respective areas of responsibility will require a different emphasis for a service than for a product. *However, the management of a quality system for higher profits involves the same fundamental principles for a service business as for a business that manufactures a product.*

Conclusion to Managing Quality for Higher Profits

Higher profits are the benefit of controlling a product's quality. This was clearly demonstrated by the case studies contained in Part III. To control a product's quality requires the presence of a quality system which can competently manage definite areas of responsibility. A detailed discussion of these areas of responsibility was the subject matter of Part II. Quality systems that can capably manage these areas possess common traits which can be built into the systems. These traits were identified and discussed in the concluding chapter of Part III. *In net, product quality can be controlled by competent management. The result is enhanced profits. For service businesses, the considerations for controlling the quality of the service so as to embellish profits are very similar to those for a product.* This topic was covered in Part IV.

The key to controlling quality so that it will yield substantial profits is the effective development and maintenance of a technically sound quality system. It is doubtful that any highly successful quality system would not in some way include the use of the total quality cost concept, or its equivalent, since it incorporates several very beneficial virtues:

1. It translates quality jargon into a language—money—familiar to general management. This can greatly assist in gaining top management understanding of and commitment to quality. This can also facilitate the authorization of resources needed to develop and manage a profitable quality system.

2. It provides a common denominator—money—for expressing different aspects of quality options and for comparing the various options. Contrast the ease with which a decision can be made to purchase $10,000 of equipment to save $25,000 per year of failure costs versus purchase of the same $10,000 of equipment to reduce the failure level from 0.2 percent to 0.1 percent.

3. It provides documentation in monetary terminology of intangible market failures. Otherwise, this real and sometimes very large cost of lost profit can be in-

189

visible to management, since it does not routinely appear in accounting reports.

4. It enables a priority to be assigned to each major quality failure category based on its total monetary cost. This can greatly aid the decision-making process regarding the allocation of resources to reduce failure costs.

5. The total cost of the quality system, T, can be directly compared to profits. This comparison can provide both quality and general management with perspective as to the scope of their quality system. Changes in T with time can provide an excellent measure of the performance of the overall quality system and its integral parts.

The total quality cost concept involves managing the total quality cost (T) to its optimum value (T_0). For a handful of select companies the designation of T_0 as the optimum is a misnomer. For these very rare and very fortunate businesses, the real optimum quality cost is less than T_0. This takes place only when the control of variability is so exceptionally outstanding as to actually become a, or the, reason for purchasing their offering(s). To acquire a reputation of this magnitude usually requires the management of a continuously outstanding quality system over many, many years. This type of reputation can be of enormous profit value, especially in a market in which it is difficult to distinguish any one brand or any one service as being dominant in degree of excellence. When this situation exists, the optimum total quality cost is given by T_0 minus the credit for increased sales due to outstanding control of variability. Although this credit may be even more difficult to quantify than its opposite, intangible market failure costs, it can be extremely valuable.

Quality systems can and should be managed by dollars and sense. To develop and maintain a profitable quality system does usually necessitate a substantial cash investment. As with any worthwhile investment, the expected benefit must justify the cash outlay. *When top management comprehends that increased profit is the benefit from an effective quality system, they will want to make the necessary investment.*

Appendix A FACT

A discussion of the total quality cost concept was contained in Chapter 1. A discussion of each of the basic areas which require effective management so that product variability can be adequately controlled was the primary subject matter of Part II. Included was a discussion for each area of the numerous factors which must be competently and thoroughly analyzed and sufficient actions implemented in order for the respective area to be effectively controlled. The purpose of this appendix is to present a technique for combining this type of factor management with the total quality cost concept so as to yield a potentially powerful "weapon" for assisting in the development of quality systems which are capable of approximating optimization of the total quality cost from the moment manufacturing operations begin. This "weapon" will be designated as "FACT": Factor Analysis for Controlling T, the total quality cost. This acronym is appropriate, because the more factual the data and information used in the factor analysis, the more precisely can the optimum T be approximated. It has already been demonstrated that the difference between the actual value and the optimum value of T can profoundly influence profits. FACT appears to me to possess the potential for successful application to entire projects. However, to date its application, although successful, has been limited to portions of projects. Therefore, the fundamentals of FACT will be presented factually without much commentary. The reader is invited to judge its merits for himself or herself.

In general, FACT involves the management of each factor (included in the respective areas of responsibility as discussed in Part II) as it applies to each designated subsystem of the total manufacturing process. Division of the overall manufacturing system into subsystems is entirely at the discretion of the manufacturer in order to facilitate the use of FACT. Individual operations or groups of operations can be designated as subsystems. Warehouse, laboratory, or utility operations can be designated as subsystems. For each subsystem, all of the pertinent factors should be managed so as to practically prevent potential quality failure costs for the respective subsystem.

The application of FACT should start simultaneously with the initial design effort for a product. We shall now consider the three-step FACT application to a new or improved product during its *development phase*.

1. *Step 1 is at the earliest practical time to estimate the total annual failure cost due to each manufacturing subsystem.* (A 1-year interval permits comparison to annual profits, and it is a convenient time frame to use.) In order to do this for any particular subsystem, estimates are needed for:

   a. The number of chances for error annually. This can be determined based on the expected annual production volume. For the JEBB case studies, 2500 150,000-pound batches were required annually to fill the 500 million bottles annually produced. For the process subsystem, each batch presented an "opportunity" for a failure(s). Similarly, each of the 500 million 12-ounce bottles of the JEBB product presented an "opportunity" for a failure(s) during the packaging operation subsystem.

   b. The frequency of occurrence of each kind of failure (e.g., tight caps, cracked caps, or oil in product). Until data from test runs are in hand, whatever other sources are available should be utilized. Data from production of a similar product utilizing similar equipment and procedures can be valuable. A thorough and comprehensive analysis by competent and experienced personnel considering each factor as it applies to each manufacturing subsystem can be quite helpful for predicting potential failures. Lacking any useful information, an educated guess will suffice until something better becomes available.

   c. The fraction of each kind of failure which will be detected internally. A manufacturer can estimate this by considering planned appraisal measures versus each kind of failure which might occur. For example, if a producer evaluates every batch of strawberry jelly for taste before it is filled into jars, it is highly likely that all failures owing to a batch of this product not adhering to its product specification for taste will be detected internally, before the product is shipped.

   d. The cost per occurrence for each type of internal failure. This can be estimated by planning in advance the actions to be taken if certain types of failures occur. To illustrate, the jelly producer mentioned above might plan to blend any off-quality batches at 20 percent into new batches. It is then easy to estimate that the cost of this internal failure would be five times the cost to blend part of the bad batch into one new one.

e. The average cost per market failure for each defect classification; that is, $\overline{MF}_{cd}$, $\overline{MF}_{sd}$, and $\overline{MF}_{yd}$. Methods for estimating these values were discussed in Chapter 6.

Step 1 concludes by combining the above data and information so as to calculate the expected total annual failure cost due to each manufacturing subsystem. For any particular subsystem, items **a** and **b** above determine the annual number of each kind of failure. The use of **c** divides these into those failures which will be internally discovered and those which will ultimately end up in the market. The use of **d** and **e** enables a monetary value to be attached to each of the two types of failures (internal and market). The sum of these two costs provides an estimate for the annual failure cost due to the particular subsystem.

2. *Step 2 requires no further action for any manufacturing subsystem which exhibits a negligible total annual failure cost by Step 1. For each subsystem which does demonstrate a significant total annual failure cost by Step 1, Step 2 is to introduce all preventive and appraisal measures which possess at least a reasonable chance of economically reducing the total failure cost for that subsystem.* In other words, the total annual failure cost should be pragmatically minimized to the extent of incorporating even quality measures with questionable ability to economically reduce failure costs. If it later turns out that a measure of this type did not possess the needed ability, it should be deleted. (The logic for taking this type of approach was covered in Chapter 9.)

Step 2 should be completed by obtaining the *estimated total annual quality cost (T_E) for the entire manufacturing system.* This is obtainable by adding the estimated annual cost of all preventive and appraisal measures to the total annual failure cost. The total annual failure cost is the sum of the estimated failure costs for all subsystems.

3. *Step 3 is to reapply steps 1 and 2 each time that more accurate and/or reliable information becomes available.* In general, steps 1 and 2 should be reapplied any time that improved information pertaining to the anticipated production volume, failure rates, the percentage or number of failures which will be detected internally, or the cost per occurrence of a failure type is obtained.

This concludes the discussion of FACT prior to the start-up of manufacturing operations.

Attention will now be focused on the application of FACT for controlling the total quality cost once actual production has started. During the start-up, an appropriate number of competent personnel should be made available to rapidly address and eliminate any unanticipated failure costs which surface. (We have previously discussed in detail the vital importance of product quality during a new or improved product's market introduction.) A time interval should be selected as the basis for a formal quality cost review. This review should be scheduled at the earliest practical time following start-up, but it must allow for a sufficient time period so as to be representative of product quality. For this time period, T should be obtained: $T = P + A + IF + MF$. P, A, and IF should be available from internal accounting records. MF can be obtained by combining (a) quality assurance data monitoring the level of "as-shipped" failures for crucial, serious, and other pertinent defect classifications, (b) available data regarding in-transit, insidious, and in-use failures, (c) the production volume during the time frame, and (d) the best available values for $\overline{MF}_{yd}$. To facilitate its utility, T should be prorated so as to be expressed as the total failure cost, T_1, based on a 1-year production volume. This enables the direct comparison of T_1 versus T_E, the *estimated* total annual quality cost.

If T_1 is approximately equal to T_E, *and* if the failure costs for the individual manufacturing subsystems are about as expected, T is probably close to its optimum value. This is because the implementation of additional economically justifiable quality measures for those functions which showed significant failure costs should already have been considered by FACT, step 2, before start-up. On the other hand, if T_1 is significantly greater than FACT's (estimated) T_E, or if some individual subsystems demonstrate higher-than-expected failure costs, the first action should be to conduct an audit to ensure that planned preventive and appraisal measures were actually being carried out in the intended manner. If the audit reveals that the planned P&A measures were as intended, then all subsystems exhibiting a higher-than-expected failure cost must be speedily reevaluated for economically justifiable quality measures to decrease the respective failure costs. Once it is established that T_1 is approximately at the estimated value T_E and that failure costs for each manufacturing subsystem are about as expected, the question of whether P&A costs are excessive should be asked. However, as demonstrated in the case studies of Part III, the effort to delete P&A measures should proceed with utmost caution.

Even after the total quality cost has been optimized, determination of the actual total quality cost should continue to be performed at regular time intervals in order to quickly detect any significant changes.

Appendix B
Glossary of
Abbreviations

A	The total cost for appraisal measures for the entire manufacturing operation
cd	Crucial defect
F	The total cost of quality failures for the entire manufacturing operation: $F = IF + MF$
IF	The total cost of internal failures for the entire manufacturing operation
MF	The total cost of market failures for the entire manufacturing operation
$\overline{MF}_{cd}$	The average market failure cost of a unit with a crucial defect
$\overline{MF}_{sd}$	The average market failure cost of a unit with a serious defect
P	The total cost for preventive measures for the entire manufacturing operation
P_C	The cost for a continuing (repetitive) preventive measure(s)
P_T	The cost for a temporary (one-time) preventive measure(s)
P+A	The combined cost of preventive plus appraisal measures for the entire manufacturing operation
Q	The total quality cost expressed as a fraction of profits: $Q = \left(\dfrac{T}{\text{profits}}\right)$
sd	Serious defect
T	The total cost of quality for the entire manufacturing operation: $T = P + A + IF + MF$

195

T' The apparent "total" cost of quality for the entire manufacturing operation when intangible market failure costs are ignored

T_E The estimated total cost of quality for the entire manufacturing operation based on 1 year of sales volume

T_0 The optimum value of T: the optimum total cost of quality for the entire manufacturing operation

T_1 T prorated so as to be based on the annual production volume

Index